California's Golden Years

California's Golden Years:
When Government Worked and Why

William T. Bagley

Berkeley Public Policy Press
Institute of Governmental Studies
University of California, Berkeley
2009

Library of Congress Cataloging-in-Publication Data

Bagley, William T.
  California's golden years : when government worked and why / William T.
  Bagley.
    p. cm.
  ISBN 978-0-87772-434-6
  1. California--Politics and government--1951- I. Title.
  JK8735.B34 209
  979.4'053--dc22

                                                                    2009025356

Acknowledgments

My grateful thanks:

• For generous help in publication, to the California Water Association, investor owners of many of California's water service utilities. They serve the public by serving water; they are water stewards, a noble calling;

• For support and coordination of this publication, to the University of California's Institute of Governmental Studies;

• For love and support over all these years, to Diane Bagley and my family. Someone once said—"Married to Bill for 45 years—Saint Diane!"

William T. Bagley
2009

Contents

Illustrations   xi

Foreword   xiii

Introduction   1

Part I—Just Some Characters   11
1. Willie Brown   13
2. Sam Yorty   15
3. Richard Nixon   17
4. Pat Nixon   19
5. Jesse Unruh, Jack Veneman, Leon Panetta, and Snow in   20
     Modesto
6. George Deukmejian—A Gem   24
7. The Birth of the Young Turks   26
8. The Legislature Grows Up—Even Sends a Delegation to   28
     Martin Luther King, Jr.'s Funeral
9. Pat Brown—Great Governor   31
Part II—What Happened   33
1. Legislative Golden Years   35
2. How We Built California As We Know It Today   37
3. Problems of the Golden Years   40
4. The Results of Reform   41

Part III—*Capitol Morning Report* Items   47
1. Phil Burton Saves Ronald Reagan   49
2. University Funding   52
3. Arnold Schwarzenegger and Ronald Reagan   58
4. Ronald Reagan's Real Record   63
5. Initiatives   68
6. Fundraisers: Dollars Instead of Dinners   72
7. Every Night is Saturday Night   73
8. Ideologues and Then Moderates   76
9. Redistricting   78
10. What Happened to Moderation and Compromise?   81

11.	Infrastructure—No Longer Golden	84
12.	Gerald Ford Remembered Upon His Demise	86
13.	Earl Warren and Arnold Schwarzenegger	91

Part IV—The Way Things Got Done 95

1.	Train Trips	96
2.	People Who Play Together Stay Together	97
3.	Still on the Subject of Card Games: We Got Smart	99
4.	About John Harmer and Howard Thelen	100
5.	The Ten Commandments—Are They Divisible?	101
6.	The Rumford Fair Housing Act	103
7.	Reflections on Jesse Unruh and "The Lockup"	106
8.	A Little Background to the Rise of Ronald Reagan and the Right Wing	109
9.	How Ronald Reagan Became Governor of California	114
10.	How Pat Brown Smeared George Christopher and How This Came Back to Haunt Him and Change History Forever	115
11.	The First Few Sour Days of Reagan's Governorship	117
12.	On Some of Ronald Reagan's Inner Circle	119
13.	Republican Speaker Bob Monagan Confronts Republican Governor Ronald Reagan—Plus, Passage of CEQA	122
14.	Reagan's Tax Revision and the 1970s Surplus	124
15.	How Income Tax Withholding Built the Governor's Mansion	126
16.	The $2 Billion Reagan Tax Package—How the Bill is Packaged and Jarvis Ruins Home Rule	129
17.	Tax Reform as a Continual Process	131
18.	Welfare Reform Negotiations, 1971, and How Ronald Reagan Participated in Felonies	133
19.	One Whacky but Relevant Election of 1966	136
20.	Why Run for State Controller?	138
21.	The 1974 Election and How It Led to Gray Davis Becoming Governor	139
22.	How Ronald Reagan Consolidated Turmoil and Becalmed the Body Politic	142
23.	Campaign Contributions Prior to the Passage of Proposition 9 —1974	145
24.	More on How Cash Cows Spilled Their Milk Prior to PAC Days in Sacramento	147

25. School Desegregation Guidelines—Another Attempt to Show   150
    that Some GOP Members Believed in Social Progress
26. Republican Fortunes in the Assembly in the Tidal Wave of   152
    Jesse Unruh's Democratic Stronghold
27. One of the Downsides to a Professionalized Legislature   154
28. Underscoring Again How Proposition Nine Has Created   155
    Precisely What it Was Designed to Eradicate – The
    Proliferation of Campaign Contributions and Expenditures
29. Whither Goes the GOP? To Withering Away?   157

Part V—There is Life after the Legislature   161
1. A Tiny Slice of Life as Chairman of the Commodity Futures   162
    Trading Commission
2. Throwing Red Tape Into the Potomac – Literally   163
3. How Jimmy Carter Tried to Shoo Me Out of the CFTC   165
4. How I Got Appointed to CFTC in the First Place   168
5. The Commodity Futures Trading Commission   169
6. The Birth of the CFTC   171

Postscript: A Unique Honor   176

Afterword: The Hon. John T. Knox   179

Biography   185

Illustrations

1. William T. Bagley   xii
2. Willie Brown's First Golf Game   12
3. Nixon at White House   16
4. "Wonderful" George Deukmejian   23
5. We Light the Bridge   25
6. The Young Turks   27
7. Pat Brown's Last Budget—$4.6 Billion   32
8. Moderates with Senator Murphy   34
9. Early Gov. Reagan   38
10. Reagan Says Thanks   42
11. Dinners Always Bipartisan   48
12. Gov. Reagan Approves Abortion—1967   60–61
13. Gov. Reagan Endorses ERA   65
14. Reagan's $2 Billion Tax Hike   66
15. Gerald Ford for Affirmative Action   87
16. Ford Speaks for Pat Brown   88
17. A Grateful Pat Brown   89
18. Nelson Rockefeller's Plane   110
19. Rockefeller Says Thanks   112–113
20. Ronald Reagan Listens   121
21. Another Thanks from Reagan   141
22. Cash from the B of A   144
23. Greetings from President Reagan   167
24. Beware of the Legislature   174
25. The Honorable John Knox   178
26. Letter Regarding Knox Bills   181

1. William T. Bagley

Foreword

The best historians are often those who lived and made history. Bill Bagley did both. In *California's Golden Years*, Bill's first-person recollections of history are more touching, more memorable, and more thought-provoking for having lived it. Bill was and is a "mover and shaker" who actually helped move and shake California through its golden years, when "America's great experiment" enjoyed its greatest success in education, infrastructure investment, business, economic growth, and social leadership. Few people have been better prepared to "move and shake" than Bill Bagley—a University of California scholar and then a real practitioner of the art of making the system work.

Bill's insights distill the past 50 years of California's political history into a series of remembrances and vignettes that support his overriding theme for successful government—"less ideology, more deliberative and collaborative leadership," borne of working friendships and trust. He explains why and how successful government is wrought from personal relationships and trust, and by reinventing the usual legislative "sausage" into a bipartisan process that avoids the ideological partisan stalemates that can paralyze a governing legislature.

More than anything, Bill is a student of history and law. "Before thinking great thoughts," he says, "read the statute!" He has counseled elected officials and his own business clients with this admonition for years, and it has paid dividends time and again. Bill has often said,

> To the lawyer, it means start with what is on the books. To the legislator, it means actually read the proposal before careening off into seeming oratorical splendor on matters irrelevant to what is before you. Do a little research and you'll save money, time, and aggravation, gain a little wisdom and insight, and ultimately be a better public servant or private citizen.

Actively engaging in a "lessons learned" process is an important part of that process, and this book is a treasure trove of lessons learned.

There are few, if any, things more important than the production, treatment, storage, conveyance, distribution, and conservation of water. The water utility industry in California—and specifically, investor-owned regulated water utilities and their customers—is indeed fortunate that Bill

Bagley devoted a great deal of his professional time and effort to ensuring that California had an adequate supply of safe, high-quality drinking water.

One of the regulated segment's greatest achievements, in which Bill had a central role, was a years-long undertaking—upheld by the California Supreme Court—that successfully preserved the authority of the California Public Utilities Commission (CPUC) to supervise and enforce the federal and state Clean Water Acts and other water regulations.

For the better part of 20 years, Bill has helped these retail water purveyors through the legislative and regulatory complexities that are the reality of California water utilities' daily lives. He has been a great friend of the industry. For this reason, the California Water Association, the state trade group that represents those investor-owned, CPUC-regulated water utilities, is pleased to have collaborated with the Institute of Governmental Studies at the University of California, Berkeley, to help make this book possible.

CWA members are proud to have helped sponsor this publication through a gift to the University of California on behalf of University Regent Emeritus William T. Bagley, both honoring his public service and thanking him for his legal counsel. This book, of course, is a personal reflection of Bill's lessons learned; accordingly, his views are his own and do not represent those of CWA or its member companies.

A student, a legislator, a regulator, an attorney, an advocate, and now a historian—Bill was and is all of these things. So when he speaks or writes from the vantage point of nearly 60 years, observing the state's evolution and condition, Californians would do well to listen. *California's Golden Years* is a real public service, and a highly entertaining one at that.

Jack Hawks
Executive Director
California Water Association
San Francisco
February 2009

Introduction

This publication is not the product of an exhaustively researched study of the mechanics of government. It is, however, a specific hands-on recitation of 50 years of relevant governmental machinations, ranging from the major progress made in our Golden Years of California (1950–1970) devolving down to later unproductive legislative ultra partisanship and near gridlock. Be it freeways, highways, bridges, transit, water, major new university campuses, and virtually all other basic infrastructure, we are today living off public money invested during those Golden Years, by our parents and grandparents.

From fun personal vignettes to serious stories of people and politics, we give flavor to and perhaps impart a message or two derived from this informative era, up to the present time.

House Speaker Tip O'Neill said "all politics is local." No, productive politics is personal. It is an art, based upon knowledge and upon developed mutual trust and thus personal relations, very human actions and reactions, performed by the players on the governmental stage.

In this book you will read about the folks in and about our Capitol and their folklore over the last 50 years. Here you will read about the players but, more importantly, how working and playing together leads to mutual respect and trust and thus progress, tragically lacking today.

Governors

George Deukmejian—Straight arrow, no false ego, wonderful human being.

Arnold Schwarzenegger—ego, but a Republican in the mold of Nelson Rockefeller.

Ronald Reagan—very decent human being, no dark side but begins with Goldwater-position, changes, doubles budget in four years, increases tax take by 20%.

Pat Brown—the builder, great governor.

And—Jerry Brown, Pete Wilson, Gray Davis.

Speakers of the Assembly

Ralph M. Brown, Jesse Unruh, Willie Brown, Bob Monagan, Bob Moretti, and more.

Major Programs and How They Happened:

Civil Rights, Abortion Rights, CEQA—The 1960s.

The Process

Collegiality.

No capitol fundraisers but free food, booze, and some cash.

Imagine, annual free press-legislative golf tournaments. Governors, members, press—all played, lobby groups paid. Everyone won a prize! We played together.

Compare

Politics and physics are similar—vacuums attract; see what the vacuums have wrought.

Read How

Read how new "reform" ruined the ability to govern, and read about an occasional felony or two . . . or more.

Read how the progression toward partisan gridlock may be tracked, cause and effect, as follows: Repeal of cross filing (1959); Proposition 9, political reform (1974); Proposition 13 (1978); Term Limits Initiative (1990); redistricting (2001). And, note the adverse effect of the initiative process and, ironically, the need for a corrective initiative.

The rise of "reform" has led to the demise of problem-solving, deliberative democracy in California when members knew each other, worked together, and played together, and thus learned to trust each other—all or at least most for the common good.

Many others have written on Sacramento subjects but no one to date has related this 50 years of personal exposure—thus here are many vignettes about who was doing what to whom and why—and what was the point and the ultimate result in politics and policy of the day.

The ability to lead is rather easily defined: achieve a civil consensus, produce results, and thus govern. Easily said. Is there a theme to be developed from the following commentary and recitations? Try this: government works well if it is fun for all involved who enjoy working and producing results together.

Also portrayed is the tyranny of political ideologues, the insanity of the extreme left and right and the disarray caused by both phony and misdirected reforms and ballot initiatives that have passed.

Before "reforms," we all ate together, worked together, and played together. All night card games in lobbyists' available hotel suites, and committees the next day. But we knew each other, learned to trust those who were worthy, and we governed through civility, camaraderie, and concern. There were no partisan aisles. People who play together, stay together. That all stopped because of ostensible political reform. Gone are the little bipartisan dinners, replaced by big dollars, because of "reform." Abstinence does not make the heart grow fonder; instead, it interferes with the real human part of governmental processes.

Apologies to the state Senate for lack of commentary—I was not there. However, it is acknowledged that the Senate was and to some degree remains the more quiet, civil, and deliberative body. Similarly, there were no partisan aisles prior to reform. The President Pro-Tem of the Senate was elected by the entire body, more or less by consensus. Club-like friendships prevailed, but admittedly included major lobbyists as "members" of the club.

Though we do glorify these Golden Years, there were some inglorious and ugly downsides. These years were the end years of a freewheeling legislature—an atmosphere, however, that actually added to the progress then made. But there were 20 or so legislators who lived on the then $500 per month stipend plus the $20 per diem and leftover campaign contributions.

At least one San Francisco assemblyman jacked-up his car to run the odometer, getting 15 cents "per mile" in his garage. Other members would fly back and forth all day to overlapping distant interim committee meetings amassing more mileage, at 15 cents per mile, far above the then fare. Some few had permission to sign a lobbyist's name on restaurant tabs. Another San Francisco member would just take a dozen or more cigars, stuffed in his pockets at each weekly "moose-milk" open house luncheon. So cheap. And there were some cash transactions. One lobbyist bought rolls of stamps from some legislators who promptly obtained more free stamps from the Rules Committee. And of course you could then pocket leftover campaign contributions.

The membership makeup to some extent was representative of the constituency. Of 120 members, one could conclude that there were about 10 drunks, dullards, and cheap crooks—mostly the same 10. Then there were 10 or so complete phonies. The remainder were all good, caring people, about 20 or 30 of whom were superior—great legislators. Significant salary and expense increases have relieved the dependency on freebies but some of those old percentages remain, probably always will. Members used to know who they were before "term limits."

Today, the legislature is a regulated industry. In addition to massive FPPC regulation of campaigns, their formation, their committees, their advertising, their contribution and expenditure limits and reporting requirements, one must report assets, income, gifts, and be subject to fines as a contributor or recipient, all subject in turn to a massive accounting bureaucracy. Has that "reform" created a better legislature?

All of this "reform" has led to the "virtually unregulated independent expenditure committee" issuing massive hit pieces, without any real identification or source of funds—enjoying the First Amendment with impunity.

In Kevin Starr's *California*, the former state librarian and premier historian writes in 2007:

> Between 1942 and 1966, during the gubernatorial administration of (Earl) Warren, Goodwin Knight, and Edmund G. "Pat" Brown, two Republicans and one Democrat, progressivism characterized state government during a period of extraordinary growth. Despite their differences, Democrats and Republicans saw sufficiently eye-to-eye to build the infrastructure—schools, colleges, and universities; freeways, roads, and bridges; public buildings and public programs of every sort—serving the rise of postwar California. For a later generation, caught in partisan turmoil and gridlock, the Warren-Knight-Brown years of confident creation seemed a golden age of vision and consensus in which Democrats and Republicans alike had held a shared membership in the Party of California.

The journalist Peter Schrag, a veteran observer of California politics, made a similar observation in his book, *California: America's High-Stakes Experiment*:

> In the generation after World War II, California, always well endowed in its climate and natural beauty, became an exemplar not only for its universities and its huge investment in schools, parks, roads, and water systems but also for the modern, professional government that the state established to oversee that investment. Its progressive social policies—the open housing and other civil rights laws and perhaps the most liberal abortion law of its time (signed by Ronald Reagan in 1967)—were enacted under both Republican and Democratic governors, among them Earl Warren,

Goodwin Knight, Pat Brown, and Reagan himself, and by legislators of both parties. Now, forty years on, they seem almost quaint. At the time they were powerful innovations. Later . . . things had descended into ugly and spiteful partisanship.

Why the disintegration? Because then, we learned to know each other. Before term limits, we ate and played together and thus we trusted each other. There were bipartisan lunches and dinners, traveling interim study committees with informal lobby-hosted events, all of which were made illegal by "political reform." Now, there are big partisan high-dollar events instead of bipartisan dinners.

Post-Proposition 9 and 13 and after a generation of political negativism—30 years later—fourth graders in California were vying with fourth graders in Mississippi for the dubious distinction of being the worst readers in the nation. The most recent poll ratings of the legislature: 11% approval, in 1969 our legislature was voted "best in the nation." What happened? Read on.

* * *

To put the Golden Years in context, an overview of operations—the *modus operandi*—of the legislature prior to "reforms" is in order. Recall California's population totaled near 10 million in 1950. Legislators were paid $100 per month, raised by public vote to $500 in the early '50s when annual budget sessions were also adopted. General Sessions were then constitutionally limited to 180 calendar days in the odd-numbered years with a 30-day budget session in March of the even years. This continued until 1966—a constitutional amendment instituted general annual sessions, and salaries were set at $16,000 per year. By then our population neared 20 million. We were not Idaho in the '50s and '60s; we were a sophisticated state getting along very well, however, with a "citizen legislature."

Speaking from 1960 forward, legislative life was rather simple. By constitutional provision (still the law) members were assemblymen and senators (there was one female member of the Assembly in 1961). Members were also friends. There were no "aisles"; we did not invade another member's district, committee roll calls were rare (only if a member dared

6

to ask for one against the chairman's call). Bills could be passed without a quorum by chairman's edict, if no one objected. Committee staff provided bill analyses as did the legislative analyst for money bills. But there were no young staff-written caucus positions on bills—members actually voted in committee and on the floor on into the '80s on their own volition! Party-line votes were rare, resulting only from voted caucus positions—perhaps four or five times a year. Amazing compared to today, and very, very sad.

Until 1967, members had just one Capitol secretary, only during session, and one district office secretary full time, plus district office rent and a $150 per month stipend. No other extraneous staff. Other than committee chairman staff, offices were closed upon adjournment. Post-1967, all assemblymen had one administrative assistant, plus a full-time Capitol secretary. (Of course the Speaker could "give" members more staff selectively.) But no plethora of chiefs of staff, spokespersons, schedulers, etc., existed. Assemblyman Alan Pattee (R. Monterey), a Harvard grad and successful dairyman, used his $150 per month stipend to pay his milker, proclaiming "I have a phone in the barn."

Most members did not have to get elected to buy groceries. Some few, those less adequate, literally lived on lobbyist largess, campaign money, mileage, and per diem. (Recall contributors did not have to report contributions, and the excess was yours.) Interestingly, travel was reimbursed at 15 cents per mile even for a Washington, D.C., flight—far beyond the then ticket cost. You could pocket about $600 "profit" if the Speaker approved D.C. travel!

But most members had businesses, stores, dairies, sold insurance, and the majority practiced law. They went to their districts to earn a living, and at least until lobby dollars flowed, to raise campaign money. As will be discussed, there were no fundraisers in Sacramento prior to "reform."

"Cross Filing" existed—candidates filed in both party primaries—until legislatively repealed in 1959. Under that system, a member could be nominated by both parties. That led to a moderate, less partisan membership and a lack of ideologue-caused gridlock. There was a Democratic Party call, joined by the League of Women Voters, for "party responsibility," i.e., adhering to party platforms and positions, which led to the repeal of cross filing and more partisanship, when the Democratic majority took control (only the second time in 60 years) in 1959.

In government, the process is the most important product. During these Golden Years, California, like many other states, had a workable process not dictated by partisanship. It had major faults, primarily caused by members without earned income existing on lobby largess, and others influenced by simple lobby friendships. But compare today, when instead of free meals and a few goodies, members collectively can extract up to $100,000 a day in fundraisers in Sacramento. Is the system, this "reformed" process, a better way to govern 37 million Californians than what we had to govern over 20 million during the Golden Years? A massive flow of dollars rather than just free bipartisan dinners—we will discuss all of that.

"It is curious that physical courage should be so common in the world but moral courage so rare." —Mark Twain.

Twain's salient observation has become almost intrinsic to the California Legislature, particularly the Assembly where voting is now a rote mechanical exercise. Caucus staff-written positions, directing committee and floor votes, have replaced individual thoughtful votes with blind unanimous partisan voting blocks, routinely cast. *A culture has evolved whereby new members seemingly think that is what they are supposed to do.* This culture is the result of the imposition of partisan "aisles" (1979), the passage of term limits, and the adoption of ultra-partisan district boundary lines. Members today react in disbelief when told, in the prior freer era, there were no party staff-dictated voting sheets, only rare full caucus meetings mostly on budget matters, and ongoing partisan block voting simply did not exist. Though philosophical, partisan and district-based pressures certainly were present, longer serving less partisan members developed their own voting patterns. Imagine!

Today the wise lobbyist tries to corral the (young) caucus staffer rather than lobbying the member. Members should feel insulted but apparently are relieved.

Solution: What is desperately needed is a "problem-solving caucus" where members can gather in bipartisan forums to discuss long-range programs and solutions—not unlike a super select committee—but that will never occur in today's dysfunctional atmosphere, particularly in the novice-inflicted Assembly bereft of bipartisan friendships. Cooperative bipartisan leadership is needed to develop a new problem-solving culture. There is meaning to an old Alaskan saying about leadership: "The nice thing about being the lead dog is the scenery changes all the time." The political landscape needs to change and so do term limits.

Unfortunately, major obstacles virtually prohibit progress: (1) Heavily partisan-drawn districts force members to vote strict party line. (2) Their planned progression to the now ultra-partisan open Senate seat (opened because of term limits) reinforces the need to create an Assembly record of ultra-partisan votes. Members are trapped in this culture.

Former Governor Jerry Brown recently recanted part of his 1974 Proposition 9 reform, saying to me, "Bring back Moose Milk." That every-Thursday lobby-sponsored free and fancy hotel luncheon open to all legislators and constitutional officers could not operate today under Jerry's law. But it could be recreated if the Democratic and Republican leadership of both Houses would simply pool some of their lobby-donated campaign largesse and host a weekly bipartisan luncheon open to all. Imagine!

Part I—Just Some Characters

2. *Willie Brown, then an assemblyman and later the legendary Speaker, at his first golf game, part of the annual press corps/legislative tournament. From left to right, Brown,* Los Angeles Times *reporter Jerry Gillam, and Bagley. Assemblyman Jack Knox, also a member of the foursome, took the picture, circa 1967. All free, courtesy lobby groups.*

1. Willie Brown

Willie Brown, later the mayor of San Francisco and ongoing *bon vivant*, cast his first vote as a newly installed freshman in the legislature on the first roll call on the first day of the 1965 session. He and fellow freshmen John Burton and Bill Stanton voted to unseat sitting Democratic Speaker Jesse Marvin Unruh! Jesse had opposed the CDC, the very liberal California Democratic Council, which was headed by future U.S. Sen. Alan Cranston. Willie was shunned and shunted off to political purgatory, given the smallest office in the Capitol by Unruh's Rules Committee, and assigned an irrelevant committee—Agriculture.

Later, there was a wonderful group who played poker every Monday night in a lobbyist's hotel suite, sometimes all night. We would wash, shower, order breakfast, sign the lobbyist's name, and go straight to the Ways and Means Committee on Tuesday mornings, without sleep. When Willie became chairman of Ways and Means in 1971, he changed the committee meetings to Wednesdays!

Incidentally, Willie ran Ways and Means very "efficiently." We did not have roll call votes in committee in those good old days, and quorums meant very little. The chairman asked for an oral vote and proclaimed the results, rarely challenged. The system worked. Folks were either trusted or tolerant.

My first conversation with Willie took place on the floor in early 1965. Knowing that as an attorney I knew some San Francisco business folks, he described his law practice as one representing "pimps, prostitutes, and other purveyors." Willie said to me, "Find me some civil law clients. I want to go uptown." I made many suggestions to lobbyists to find him some landlord clients, some business transactions, transfers of liquor licenses, and so on. But all to no avail. Willie went uptown anyway, all the way and all on his own.

Times have changed in many other ways. By the early '70s, former Speaker Bob Monagan (R-Tracy) was Assistant Secretary of the U.S. Department of Transportation and Bob Beverly (R-Manhattan Beach) was now minority leader. Jerry Lewis (R-Redlands)—later chairman of the

U.S. House Appropriations Committee—was Beverly's roommate during our six-month sessions.

Willie Brown had introduced his first "Consenting Adults Act" repealing all criminal code prohibitions re sodomy and other sexual acts (except bestiality). The bill, later to become law, received only 18 Democratic votes and originally just three from Republicans—Bill Bagley, Bob Beverly, and Jerry Lewis (Beverly and Lewis shared an apartment). Roommate Lewis came running up to the Assembly Desk shouting to Beverly—"One of us gotta change our vote." Willie's bill was defeated that year, garnering only 20 votes out of the needed 41.

2. Sam Yorty

This is a fun story. Sam Yorty had been an assemblyman from southern California. He started out as very liberal, a '30s lefty, and then became more conservative at the end of his career as the mayor of Los Angeles.

When he was in the Assembly in the late '30s and '40s, he was something of a renegade. There was a lot of red-baiting going on, and this then liberal assemblyman from Los Angeles was churning things up in the legislature. One of his supposed antics ended up being named after him.

Prior to the early 1950s, before the Capitol Annex was built, there were very few offices for members. Private conversations often took place in the men's room, a semi-private atmosphere. Perhaps there were other people in the stalls, so most people were wary.

But Yorty used to go into one of the stalls and sit on the throne with his legs up. This was his way of deliberately trying to sneak in on private conversations!

By the time I got to the legislature, in 1961, if you went into the bathroom during the session when things were going on, talking to your colleagues, you'd do what we called the "Yorty Stoop." You'd get down almost to your hands and knees to see if someone else was sitting on the throne with legs up and ears open.

You didn't just lean over and look for legs. You'd get way down and look to see if someone was sitting in the Yorty position. To this day, that procedure is still known to a few of us as the "Yorty Stoop."

Twenty years later, when Sam Yorty was mayor of Los Angeles, he would stage a series of birthday events for himself similar to campaign fundraisers, except the bottom of the invitation read, "Donations are gifts to Sam Yorty." No limit, no reporting, no tax. Those were the days!

3. Bagley and President Richard Nixon. Bagley thought Nixon was "very bright but introspective."

3. Richard Nixon

After suffering a very close defeat to John F. Kennedy in 1960, Richard Nixon joined a major Los Angeles law firm, bought a house in Beverly Hills (30 Martins Place), and began his 1962 campaign for governor of California. The far right—emerging from the 1958 Knowland debacle and later the heart of the 1964 Goldwater Movement—opposed Nixon and sponsored Assembly Minority Leader Joe Shell, from Bakersfield, who in the June 1962 primary received 33% of the vote against Nixon.

Nixon had to prove he was interested in California, but at every campaign stop he was asked about the Cuban Missile Crisis and other world events. The media, particularly the *Los Angeles Times*, would portray Nixon as not concerned with state issues. The campaign was headquartered on Wilshire. Bob Haldeman, who was later White House chief of staff, was the campaign manager. Ron Ziegler, who was later the White House press secretary, literally ran the mimeograph machine producing daily news releases.

Early in 1962, needing to connect with Sacramento, Haldeman contacted two fresh-faced freshman members of the Assembly—Hugh Flournoy and myself. Flournoy, a Republican from Claremont, was asked to lead research. I was asked to travel with "the boss" in the primary—by car, press bus, and private plane. Freshman Assemblymen Bob Monagan and Jack Veneman later joined Nixon in campaign issue discussions. These four were the "Young Turks" in the legislature.

Nixon can best be described as very bright but introspective, certainly not an animated out-going "pol," a very quick study but very few jokes and little laughter. Some of his off-hand comments are worth recounting here. "From the courthouse to the statehouse" is a phrase used in other states; we would tell Dick to say "Capitol" in California.

On many early mornings, driver Sandy Quinn or Ron Ziegler and I would pick up the candidate on the way to the day's events. Dick would say, "What is on for today, another 'broad-butt' event?" We would explain that (for good reason) the Federated Republican Women of California were known as "the broad bottoms!"

17

A memory regarding political advice: Coming back from a day in Long Beach and San Pedro (visiting and shaking hands in a fish plant production line), we were stuck in 5 p.m. Harbor Freeway traffic. Dick Nixon in the front seat, later White House loyal personal aide Rosemary Woods and I in the back—with my knee against the back of the front seat. Nixon is quiet, smelling slightly of fish, and introspective. Suddenly he turns, slaps me on the knee, and says, "Bill, never go on television when you are tired." Certainly he was recalling his loss of the presidency and his loss in the closing Nixon/Kennedy debate less than two years before.

That evening we arrived back in Los Angeles at the Statler Hilton hotel. The candidate must have been feeling better—in an elevator two men stared at Nixon but soon reached their floor. Nixon shouted, "Give me a vote." "We are from Iowa," was the reply. Nixon's last words as the elevator door closed: "Then organize call girls for Nixon tonight." That is the only joke or frivolity that I can recall in three months of traveling with "the boss," but the two Iowans must have told the story many times.

Nixon of course lost to Governor Pat Brown in November, and famously told the press, postelection Wednesday morning at the Ambassador Hotel, "Now you won't have Nixon to kick around anymore!" This was a fascinating way for a young freshman assemblyman to spend almost three months, after adjournment of the then one-month budget-only session in March of 1962.

Speaking of politics, prior to my 1960 election and while standing at the end of a group photo, Governor Goodwin J. Knight advised: "Bill, put your arm over on my shoulder—that way they won't cut you out." I have employed that ploy ever since, for 50 years.

4. Pat Nixon

One day we visited Pat's childhood home in Yorba Linda. It was being dedicated. It was like the old wooden houses on D Street in San Rafael. We all stood on the little wooden porch and made an event of it.

She was quiet, but she did speak that day in eloquent paragraphs, not flowery, but eloquent and sincere. Humble may be too strong a word, but she had a quality of humility.

We were always on a press bus or in a private car or a private plane, a four-person plane. Dick would be in the front with the pilot and Pat and I would be in the back. By that time, she was accustomed to being a politician's wife.

She was thin, frail. But she was the strength. She was loyal. She knew what we were doing. We were running for governor and, by God, she was there. She was always there, a quiet stalwart.

She was a gracious hostess. She would always say, "Thank you, this is so good for Dick." I don't think Dick ever said thank you. Even later, when he was president and I would be invited to their home in San Clemente, she said, "Thank you for being here." My Gaw'd, here I've been invited to the president's house and she's thanking me.

5. Jesse Unruh, Jack Veneman, Leon Panetta, and Snow in Modesto

A very special election was held in February of 1962. Were it not for the ambitions of Jesse Unruh, then the chairman of the Ways and Means Committee—Jack Veneman could not have been elected assemblyman, and, as we shall show, Leon Panetta would not have become President Clinton's chief of staff and now director of the CIA.

When Jack was in this "sudden death" special election to represent all of Stanislaus County, Governor Pat Brown was heard to say: "It will snow in Modesto the day a Republican is elected in that county." It snowed in Modesto on Election Day—and Jack won by 1,500 votes.

Because of the dramatic switch of party control in 1958 (Pat Brown vs. Bill Knowland), Ralph M. Brown, D-Modesto, became the first Democratic Speaker of the Assembly since 1938. But by then, junior Assemblyman Jesse Unruh had made major leadership moves. Jesse became Ways and Means chairman and wanted to be Speaker. Quietly, Unruh posed to Brown the prospect of a full-time, well-paying respected position on a high court—an offer that Brown agreed to accept.

Even though there was no demonstrable need for a new court, Unruh passed legislation creating the 5th District Court of Appeal, to be located in Fresno, south of Modesto. Unruh made sure that Pat Brown would sign the bill and commit to appointing Ralph Brown to the new court in September 1961 when the legislation took effect. Thus the 1962 special election in Stanislaus County.

Also during the 1961 session, Unruh had the Assembly rules changed to allow the friendly Rules Committee to call the Assembly back as a "Committee of the Whole," thus to elect Jesse as Speaker in October 1961. Jesse did not want to risk the existence of an attractive vacancy the following January.

Jesse was a formidable and in his early speakership years an arrogant figure. He had a large presence. My young wife to-be Diane did not know Jesse and he did not know her. Sitting alone in Frank Fat's restaurant, she sees Jesse come in and looks up at him. As he walks by her he says out loud, "Don't look at me that way unless you mean it." Diane was horrified.

Jack Veneman and I had tried to recruit then U.S. Senator and Assistant Minority Leader Thomas H. Kuchel to run for governor in 1966. We flew to Washington, D.C., courtesy of one of my law clients who needed Kuchel's assistance. We met Kuchel's staff, Legislative Assistants Leon Panetta and Steve Horn. Two years later, Senator Kuchel was defeated in the Republican primary by state schools chief Max Rafferty, king of the right-wing kooks.

In the 1968 general election, former Democratic California Controller Alan Cranston defeated Rafferty and was elected to the U.S. Senate, but Richard M. Nixon was elected president. When Veneman became Undersecretary of Health, Education, and Welfare, he placed Leon Panetta as the Director of Civil Rights, all under Secretary Bob Finch, who had run the Nixon campaign as California's then lieutenant governor.

Panetta immediately began to enforce the new Johnson-era civil rights laws in the South. This directly conflicted with Attorney General John Mitchell's "southern strategy," a ploy looking to play up to southern Democratic rednecks in future elections.

John Mitchell called President Nixon one Monday in the spring of 1969. He said: "Fire that prick in the basement of HEW!"

President Nixon called Secretary Finch, and Finch relayed the order, to fire Panetta, to Undersecretary Veneman. Veneman refused, threatened to resign himself, boycotted HEW, and stayed in my visiting hotel room for three days.

On Wednesday afternoon, at 4:50 p.m., Secretary Finch arrived and reported to the Georgetown Hotel room that he, Finch, had convinced President Nixon to countermand the order. Panetta was not fired. Jack Veneman jumped up and down like a little kid, shouting, "We beat the president!"

Leon Panetta later resigned, changed his registration to Democrat, moved back home to Monterey, and ran against and beat sitting Republican Congressman Burt Talcott.

So, were it not for Jesse Unruh, Ralph M. Brown, John Mitchell, snow in Modesto, and particularly Jack Veneman, Leon Panetta would have become a successful Republican lawyer but never a Democratic congressman and then President Bill Clinton's chief of staff.

Until 2009, Panetta led the Panetta Institute, a very productive "think tank" in Monterey. Also, he was a member of the high level Iraq Study Group, also known as the Baker-Hamilton Commission, which assessed the situation in Iraq. He is now President Obama's director of the CIA.

And I should add that Jack later became counselor to Vice President Nelson Rockefeller, and Jack's daughter Ann—who Jack helped to bring to Washington in earlier years—became secretary of agriculture in the Bush II administration and is now international director of UNICEF—all because of Jesse Unruh and because it snowed in Modesto in February 1962.

4. Bagley and Governor George Deukmejian, "accomplished, unassuming, honest and loyal."

6. George Deukmejan—A Gem

A very interesting aside from the court-ordered "one man, one vote" 1966 state Senate redistricting—how George Deukmejian became governor in 1982: Of the 13 new Senate seats assigned to Los Angeles County in 1966, one was assigned to the Long Beach area, and Orange County received an additional seat or two. Arbitrarily, using odd and even district numbers, 20 new seats had two-year terms and 20 provided four-year terms. George had been assigned a four-year seat. It was then that Assemblyman Deukmejian literally traded district numbers with John Schmitz of Orange County, happily giving Schmitz the new four-year term, and George taking the new two-year numbered seat.

What forethought! George's new seat would in the future come up for reelection in off-statewide years. Thus a "free ride"—he could and did run for attorney general, lose, but keep his Senate seat, and later win another A.G. election and then run for and win the governorship. In politics there is almost nothing better than a "free ride."

I have never met a more decent human being—most accomplished, unassuming, honest, and loyal. George, now 82 years of age, and Gloria and their children are, atypically, a perfect American family.

5. We raised private money to permanently light the spans of the San Francisco-Oakland Bay Bridge. The governor threw the switch, circa 1988. Seated is Diane Bagley and Gloria Deukmejian (not shown) celebrating the 50th birthday of the bridge.

7. The Birth of the Young Turks

In November 1960, there were nine legislators elected to the freshman class, five of them Republicans: Bob Monagan, Hugh Flournoy, Jack Veneman (in 1962), Gordon Cologne, and myself.

We were known as the Young Turks—some people say the maturing Young Turks, the Old Turks of now. Those were the Republicans. The Young Turks stood for a resurgent moderate movement in the Republican Caucus in Sacramento. When we arrived in 1961, Joe Shell was Minority Leader. He was a Knowland person and in 1962, Shell ran as a "conservative" against Richard Nixon for the Republican nomination for governor, and got 33% of the vote. This probably helped create the demise of "Governor Nixon," because it was a strident campaign. The right wing accused Nixon of being a left-winger—really!

Nixon was a member of the Council on Foreign Relations, the Trilateral Commission, and similar policy groups. People of the right-wing mold would come up to me and would give me the heavy finger on the shoulder and say: "You're some kind of a liberal sympathizer because you are a friend of Nixon. He's a liberal!"

Now, it's unbelievable to say that today, but that was a fact and that was, in turn and in truth, the genesis of my becoming a very liberal Republican or, at the least, an "evangelical moderate." I couldn't stand these right-wing, bug-eyed, blithering, bigoted Birchers!

The "Young Turks," developing a cadre of like-minded members, became the forefront of a forward-looking, problem-solving band of Republican legislators in the '60s and '70s.

6. The Capitol press corps named them the "Young Turks"—moderate Republicans elected in the early 1960s who revived GOP efforts: (left to right) Bagley, Jack Veneman of Modesto, Assembly Speaker Bob Monagan of Tracy, and Hugh Flournoy of Claremont, circa 1967. Flournoy was then the state controller.

8. The Legislature Grows Up—Even Sends a Delegation to Martin Luther King's Funeral

When Jesse Unruh became Speaker of the Assembly, the legislature met in general session every other year for a constitutionally limited 180 legislative days. It was a secondary force, submissive to governors who incidentally were all Republicans during the 20th century except for Culbert Olson, 1938–1942, and now Pat Brown—Jesse would not be submissive to Pat. We were an equal branch of government! The governor had a state airplane, Jesse wanted one. He was not about to play "third fiddle" behind Pat Brown and the more powerful state Senate.

From this feeling sprung Prop. 1A, 1966, creating annual sessions and increasing the legislative stipend of $500 per month to $16,000 per year (plus per diems and mileage). Crucial to public passage of the salary provision was the concept of annual sessions.

Jesse also let the political world know that he was (we were) equal to the governor. Pat Brown had a Washington, D.C., office, Jesse opened an Assembly office to deal with Congress; when the governor was invited to events of consequence, Jesse (the Assembly) was also invited!

It was thus that in April 1968 Jesse Unruh sent his delegation to Martin Luther King's funeral in Atlanta—Assemblyman Leon Ralph (D-LA), Assemblyman Willie Brown (D-SF) with his wife Blanche, and Assemblyman Bill Bagley (R-San Rafael). (I was sent, I am sure, because of my consistent civil rights record: I had bested Willie Brown one year on the NAACP good/bad voting score card: Republican Bagley 17–1/Brown 14–2. I am still very proud of that fact, but other Republican members cast upwards of 14 "bad" votes and a low of three "good" votes. So sad.)

The funeral was a most humbling human experience. We arrived late after an all-night Delta Airline flight and the not large Ebenezer Baptist Church was full. Recognizing Willie by the door, we were escorted by a Student Non-Violent Coordinating Council usher up the fire escape, through the vestibule and onto the altar—standing next to a singing/crying church choir. We looked over those assembled: Coretta King and the family front and center; Hubert Humphrey and Thurgood Marshall to the right front row; Nelson Rockefeller, Gov. Romney, New York Mayor Lindsey together in the center, 10 rows back. The whole Kennedy clan five rows back to the right, and Dick Nixon with Wilt (the Stilt) Chamberlain and Senator Gene McCarthy behind the Kennedys, two rows back.

In retrospect it was a political event. After the ceremony and in the aisle, a gathering surrounded the Kennedys; Dick Nixon, alone, cried out "Hello Bill" to me. Gene McCarthy, also alone, reached over Nixon's shoulder and said to me—"Why don't you say hello to me?" This was surreal.

The crowd outside was somber, greeting each other "Hello brother." The march to Morehouse College for the burial began but needing our rental car to return to the airport, we drove through "Black Town" and then walked to the front of the march and then on to Morehouse College.

While driving on a rutted road passing "homes" of clapboard, some with cloth rags in place of windows, I stopped at the one and only stop sign. Willie, in the back seat of our big black Hertz Oldsmobile opened the window and shouted "Hello" to three black boys on the corner. He then said: "Bags, those kids were staring at you—they ain't never seen a white guy driving four niggers (his word) through this part of town!" We parked our car and then met up with the front of the march, joined in right behind the caisson and joyfully sang "We Shall Overcome," I for the first time.

Back to Sacramento, the new full-time legislature was obviously better suited to handle year-to-year matters (before term limits and ideological gridlock) but there were downsides. In prior years, most members had local jobs; they lived in the district with their families, dealt daily with their local people, even raised campaign dollars locally. And, having occupations or owning businesses, they did not have to get re-elected in order to buy groceries. Further, there was time for real interim committee studies around the state with members actually reading and personally reworking the actual words of draft legislation!

A further 1966 change was effected by *Silver vs. Jordan*, which mandated a "one man/one vote" reapportionment of the state Senate. Theretofore, Senate districts ranged from one senator per county (including Los

Angeles County) to a three-county district of Alpine, Mono, and Inyo comprising 15,000 people. From 1966 forward, Los Angeles County has had 13 senators.

9. Pat Brown—Great Governor

Lest we forget, Pat Brown was one of the truly great governors of California. Much will be related here about his Golden Years of programs for the state, literally building the state.

Pat cared deeply. Many years later (in the '80s) at a nonprofit board meeting where Pat and I had been chairmen, he was pounding the table: "What are we going to do for water in 2020?"

We are still wondering will environmentalists allow us to build new storage. "When the well goes dry, we value water," so said Ben Franklin. California presently risks human and economic disaster without new water storage.

Poor Pat. We used to attack him as a "profligate spender"—his last budget was $4.6 billion. In 1966, on his birthday, I wrote a check to Edmund G. Brown for $4.6 billion to cover the budget that we were holding up. Pat endorsed the check to Jesse Unruh, "without recourse."

Another quote from Pat Brown, commenting on the Eel River flood in 1965: "This is the greatest disaster since my election." In his 1966 gubernatorial race, by the way, Ronald Reagan could not identify the Eel River.

Years later in 1978, as chairman of the Commodity Futures Trading Commission, I wrote a fun personal check to Henry Jarecki, a major commodity industry leader, to "cover losses we had caused him for the year"—$24 million. An odyssey—the check was lost, traveled around New York, ended up with a *Washington Post* columnist and became a feature in the May 15, 1978 edition of *The Post*. Point of these tales is that you lose real money-earning ability while in office but government should be and was a hell of a lot of fun. Doing good is also fun, and productive.

SAN RAFAEL MAIN OFFICE
CROCKER-ANGLO NATIONAL BANK
Fourth & B Streets

NO.

SAN RAFAEL, CALIFORNIA, April 20 1966   90-1128
1211

PAY TO THE ORDER OF Edmund G (Pat) Brown $4.6 Billion

4 Billion Six hundred Million and no/100 DOLLARS

Wm. T. Bagley

7. On Gov. Pat Brown's birthday in 1966, Bagley gave him a present: a check for $4.6 billion, that year's entire state budget, which Republicans were blocking in the Assembly.

Part II—What Happened

8. *Political moderates, including Bagley, with U.S. Sen. George Murphy and Assembly Speaker Bob Monagan at a news conference in the Capitol. Note a young Pete Wilson in the rear. Front standing, Assemblymen Jerry Lewis, Paul Priolo, Bill Ketchum, and George Milias.*

1. Legislative Golden Years

Subject to a few legislative quirks, quacks, and crooks, the years 1950 to 1974 were the golden years of untarnished productive lawmaking in California.

Most part-time citizen legislators (without term limits) considered their office to be a public service—not a "job." Many were lawyers who practiced law without constant allegations of conflict of interest. A national Ford Foundation-supported group— "Legis 50"—named our legislature number one in the nation in the late 1960s. At that time, 65% of those polled "had confidence" in their state government; most recent polls put it at 11% for the legislature. So sad.

And, pre-Proposition 9, there were absolutely no morning, noon, and night fundraisers held in Sacramento. (Granted, there were—possibly still are—some one-on-one cash transactions.) But absolutely all, 100%, of those insidious $3,600—today's max—nightly Sacramento fundraisers were spawned by the 1974 passage of the mother of all reforms, Proposition 9.

Prior to the passage of Proposition 1A (so numbered to head the ballot list) in 1966, the state constitution limited sessions to 180 legislative days in the odd-numbered years with a 30-day budget session (the month of March) in between.

Earlier, there were no such budget sessions—budgets carried for two years and the "pay" had been $100 per month. This was increased, by public vote, to $500 per month in 1951.

Thus, from 1951 to 1966, legislators were paid $6,000 per year plus the going state per diem, which was $19 in 1961, while in session or at "interim hearings." The state rate at the Biltmore Hotel in Los Angeles was $8.00 per night and a flight from San Francisco to Los Angeles cost $15.00 each way on PSA, but members were given 15 cents per mile for all travel, profiting thereby.

The vast majority of legislators had their own businesses or professions. They practiced law. They ran their markets or drugstores (or spouses did during the sessions). They were insurance agents, dairymen, ranchers, funeral directors, doctors. And they were thus independent.

This group provided collective excellence to the legislature. There were a few, however, who literally lived on the petty largesse of lobbyists—cash contributions, hotel rent paid, and state mileage payments at 15 cents per mile, triple the actual cost.

And, prior to the 1978 passage of Proposition 13 and the resultant advent of Republican ideologues in the Assembly, there were no party "aisles" and no party-issued positions on bills. In the early '60s, Assemblyman (later Senator) Al Alquist (D-San Jose) and I were seated together. All his life, until passing at the age of 90, he affectionately called me "seatmate."

With the exception of rare caucus meetings, which resulted in a "caucus position," members were unfettered and actually cast their own votes. Unfortunately, this open process has devolved down to young caucus staffers issuing daily aye or no voting sheets. Members just fall in line. Party voting is the order of the day, every day. It is absolutely disgusting, when asking a member his or her position on a given bill, to watch as he or she refers to a caucus voting sheet—sometimes opening a drawer looking for the sheet.

2. How We Built California As We Know It Today

In 1940, California had a population of less than seven million people. Texas had about six-and-a-half million. Nevada had 110,000; New York 12 million. Our postwar growth is legendary. Today, we approach 38 million (and Nevada has surpassed two million). Virtually all of California's present infrastructure was built from the '30s to the '60s, a fiscally impossible feat today, while we were experiencing a "continental tilt" of population to the West.

Under the aegis of Governors Earl Warren (1943–1952), Goodwin Knight (1953–1958), and Edmund G. "Pat" Brown (1959–1966), we built the University of California campus network, new state colleges, a massive north/south water storage and transfer system, thousands of miles of interstate freeways, transit systems, and the structural backbone of literally hundreds of new cities. We also tore down our city rail systems and tore up thousands and thousands of acres of fertile farmlands.

But from the end of that era, and beginning with Governors Ronald Reagan and "Jerry" Brown (a full 16 years), we simply collapsed infrastructure construction—we are now living on the past investment of our parents, led by yesterday's leaders. From 1982 forward, Gov. George Deukmejian did reinvest in California. During his time in office, the gas tax increased from nine to 18 cents per gallon, and support for the University of California increased significantly.

Interestingly, Ronald Reagan and Jerry Brown share common blame. Governor Reagan in his early gubernatorial years just did not believe in government; Jerry Brown instead tried to govern our very way of life, propounding that "small is beautiful."

Nothing was built by the state, but the population growth continued unbounded. Today, so-called conservatives—otherwise addicted to capital investment—oppose government capital projects. Those same "conservative interests" have stymied our system of financing improvements, be it by bond or pay-as-you-go financing.

9. *Bagley shares a light-hearted moment with Gov. Ronald Reagan.*

We can now see the seeds of governmental disorder planted in the 1970s and the resultant advent of "reform"—voter reforms, legislative reforms, tax reform, welfare reform, etc.—mostly imposed by ballot initiative occurring in the past 25 years.

Note, for example:

1. Ronald Reagan's massive state tax increase caused a later (1978) massive $6 billion revenue surplus, which fueled Proposition 13, which subsequently led to the crippling of abilities to even maintain our infrastructure. It also destroyed any real semblance of self-determination by city or county government. "Home rule" has become just a homey homily.

2. The 300% disparity in AFDC payments (between California and, e.g., Mississippi) in one sense added to urban decay. The lack of a national norm virtually forced urban state migrations, i.e., to California.

3. Legislative changes and voter initiatives have eviscerated the working organs of our legislative process, all in the name of "reform." The "full-time" legislature, which now virtually prevents outside, independent earned income, the insidious Proposition 9 (1974), which also regulated conflicts and thus legislators' ability to earn a separate livelihood, the invidious Proposition 13 (1978), other assorted tax limitation proposals ending with Proposition 218 (1996), and, of course, the term limits proposition are the combined culprits.

So, beware of ideologues and reformers, often the same individuals or groups. But also note the present need to reform the reformers—the dichotomy is recognized.

3. Problems of the Golden Years

Before launching into glorification of the Golden Years—the pre-term limits era, the pre-ideologue control of caucus operations, and the pre-Proposition 9 era of bipartisan friendship, lunches, and dinners—the following should be acknowledged:

1. There were small close-knit lobby groups, which had very significant ongoing influence on leadership, based on long-term friendships or support. Understandably, powerful lobby coalitions had direct effect on Pro-Tem and Speakership elections and certainly still do at times. This was true of both labor and industry groups. Also, some committees, the whole committee met for a lobbyist dinner the night before key meetings and decisions/votes were made on bills to be heard the next day. It is not shocking that members make decisions before an oral hearing.

2. Campaigns were inexpensive generally, but contributions did arrive in cash envelopes or as cashier's checks with no traceable source—often the bank cashier's name was all that was reported to the secretary of state.

3. Though legislative leadership thrived on hard work and friendships—and thus consensus, some rank and file members (particularly in the Assembly) left a lot to be desired. Out of the 120 rooted in both houses, about 10% the same 10% overlapping at times) were drunks, frauds, and/or outright cheap crooks—plus a few just plain dullards. Then there were (probably always will be) 50 to 70 mostly pleasant folks doing their best to vote on bills, make some progress, to serve the public, and coast along enjoying their position. Then there were—hopefully still are—30 or so superlative human beings, engaged, providing leadership generally and, most importantly, working on the development of mile-post legislation in specific areas of expertise for years—but today there are only four productive years in the Assembly, then for the last two years you are a lame duck. Thus there is virtually no long-term policy development generated by the Assembly.

4. The Results of "Reform"

A. Dollars Instead of Dinners

On three successive legislative session days, randomly chosen during late February and early March 2008, one lobbyist group or one entity desiring a presence at each Capitol legislative fundraising event could have spent a total of $121,400, paying the maximum requested. For that one entity perhaps a big vote is pending, so arrange attendance at every event in force, $40,000 per day for every "event," each day. This does not happen but it would be legally, physically, and financially possible for a statewide network of contributors to do just that.

As stated on preceding pages, prior to 1974s Prop. 9, there were *no* organized event fundraisers. Lobbyists bought lunches and dinners—ecumenical (i.e., bipartisan) small gatherings and also open-house lunches for all members and constitutional officers. This was caustically called "wining and dining." Do the arithmetic—for $120,000 someone could host 10,000 bipartisan lunches at $12.00 per head or, at $20.00, 6,000 dinners. And, add to the irony: today's "events" are all partisan; party colleagues can attend but never the other party. Thus, never are all members together in an informal atmosphere, and almost never are senators and assembly men and women brought together socially. Shame on Proposition 9. Shame on "reform." Massive dollars have replaced the basically outlawed collegial dinners and thus to a great extent have replaced civility in Sacramento. Today members and candidates accept that this is the way it works.

B. Add Term Limits to Prop. 9

The rise of "reform" (Proposition 9 and term limits) and the coincident fall of bipartisanship has led to the demise of what was collegial, deliberative democracy in California—when members knew and learned to trust each other and thus produced results by working together and yes, playing together over the years. People who play together, stay together. It takes three to four years to establish these relationships and to earn trust yourself—but today in the Assembly at least 66% of your colleagues are gone, replaced after four years.

JAN 2 6 1973

State of California
GOVERNOR'S OFFICE
SACRAMENTO 95814

RONALD REAGAN
GOVERNOR

January 23, 1973

The Honorable William T. Bagley
Member of the Assembly
State Capitol
Sacramento, California

Dear Bill:

Thank you for sending the clipping. Thank
you also for giving me the opportunity that
brought about the clipping. Aren't you
impressed that the spirit of Jefferson lives
in me?

Best Regards,

RONALD REAGAN
Governor

10. In 1973, Gov. Ronald Reagan wrote to Bagley after he signed Bagley's bill to protect the confidentiality of news sources.

And after four years, you and 26 of your election-year class are relegated to the realm of lameduckdom, ineffective and looking for a new seat somewhere.

So, why bother with trust and real friendships; just sit and vote on "caucus positions" without (like eunuchs) producing any long-term legislative initiatives and programs. So very sad.

Note, it's not really their fault—the voters did it to them (us) with phony reforms and other measures that constrict real deliberative democracy.

C. Other Observers Agree:

Other knowledgeable observers state the same. Longtime *L.A. Times* reporter Bill Boyarsky and author of his new book *Big Daddy*—(2008)—states on page 16:

> It is striking how much of what is good about California—the parks, the universities, the highway system, much of the water importation and distribution system—dates from those days. California at the start of the twenty-first century is the California Unruh and the others (Govs. Warren, Knight and Pat Brown) of his generation had built half a century earlier. They were a generation of hope and optimism, men and women who had survived the Depression and the war and emerged into the bright dawn of seemingly endless possibilities.

> I would add: because they embraced common goals, free of bitter partisanship and propelled to build an ongoing consensus based upon trust built over years of service together.

Boyarsky continues:

> There have been enormous changes. . . . Leaders without a common goal struggle to appease rival interests. For example, the new symbol of California is a not a university but a prison, a monument to interest groups that have exploited the public's fear of crime.

Yes, there was a profusion of legislative pluses and thus major governmental progress in the '50s and '60s simply because of positive, not negative, political alliances. These measures were pervasive in their coverage and effect. None is subject to repeal today and few had their genesis in private economic interest lobbying. They were, instead, the product of a workable and working legislative institution—their leaders with years of knowledge and experience.

Much of this occurred long before the "one man/one vote" movement culminated with court orders: *Baker v. Carr* and *Silver v. Jordan*. California embarked upon major water transfer (north to south) and other infrastructure investment even in the face of pre-1966 Senate District apportionment, a 31–8 northern county majority with Kern County in a schizophrenic mode in between.

See the Afterward for a listing of major '60s-'70s legislation, but just one earlier example, for now, illustrative of a major positive change in the processes of government—where the process is the most important product.

The Ralph M. Brown Act (1953). Ralph, with whom I served, opened all local government boards and commission meetings for the first time, universally. Assemblyman and later Speaker Brown (D-Modesto) was chairman of the Assembly Judiciary Committee. A legislator by avocation, as is now the quaint custom, he made his living by practicing law in the Valley. In 1952 he had appeared before a local school or hospital board advocating an issue for his client. The board cast a vote in his favor; he left the meeting. The board later adjourned to an anteroom and reversed the vote, changing the minutes. Brown, with the help of then *San Francisco Chronicle* cub reporter Mike Harris and *Modesto Bee* reporter Jack Craemer (later editor/publisher of the *Marin Independent Journal*) wrote his act. The California Newspapers Association (Johnny Long, lobbyist) pushed for passage.

Early resistance such as requiring you to "sign in and state your reason for attending" (San Diego City Council, 1954) was quickly overturned in appellate courts. If governments were not to be always open, at least the processes for openness were in place. An atmosphere of openness was created. Do note later freedom of information laws, all authored by this author.

PART III—*Capitol Morning Report* Items

(Editor's note: This is a series of items written in recent years for the Sacramento-based *Capitol Morning Report*. They are reprinted with the permission of the *Capitol Morning Report*. Some of the background and information repeats what is written elsewhere in this volume.)

11. Gov. Pat Brown with friends at an always-hosted bipartisan Sacramento event5

1. Phil Burton Saves Ronald Reagan

This is a story about how the late and extremely liberal Congress-man Phil Burton saved the Republican Party, circa 1964–1965. The story begins with the Republican debacle of 1958, which took shape because California's incumbent Republican Senator, Bill Knowland, believed he could more easily ascend to the presidency from the governor's seat than from the U.S. Senate. Thus, he forced aside the moderate Republican in-cumbent, Goodwin Knight, and ran as the "right to work" candidate, leav-ing an unfunded Knight to run for Knowland's old seat in the Senate.

That crassly forced switch to the right caused a massive upheaval. Democrat Pat Brown was elected governor by a 20-point margin and the Assembly switched from an earlier 50–30 Republican to 45–35 Demo-cratic. And after the reapportionment of 1961, masterminded by the afore-mentioned Burton, who was then in the Assembly, and Assemblyman Bob Crown, it got even worse. Assembly Republicans went down to 27 seats, and in the Senate they hit a nadir of 13.

Meanwhile, the right-wing movement led by the John Birch Society was making an effort to take over the party of Lincoln. Their idea was to capture Republican nominations in the many Democratic legislative and congressional districts that Burton and Crown had created. Since winning was impossible, no Republican in his or her right mind wanted to run.

But the goal of many new nominees was not an electoral victory but party control. The year was 1964 and in that period—long since changed—the state party platform was, by government code statute, drafted by all party nominees—congressional, Senate, Assembly, and constitutional of-fices—meeting in the Assembly chambers. Note: nominees outnumbered incumbents by a two-to-one ratio.

Thus, out of committee and on to the floor came a civil rights resolu-tion to "send Negroes back to Africa." Literally, this was a direct quote from the 1878 National Republican (party of Lincoln) Party platform. Since at the hour of 6 p.m. most normal folks had left for drink and dinner, those few incumbents left on the floor were afraid this plank would pass.

Then Assemblymembers Jack Veneman, Alan Pattee, Don Mulford, and myself called for a quorum. Then U.S. Rep. Bill Maillard, presiding, ruled that a quorum was not present and adjourned the convention—without a platform. (That was also the year that Senator Barry Goldwater lost California to President Lyndon Johnson by 1.9 million votes, the biggest percentage margin to date.)

Some time later, a few of us told our convention story to Phil Burton. We mused about upcoming Republican State Committee membership meetings and the future of the Republican Party. State statutes at that time specified that Republican legislative and congressional nominees (and state constitutional office nominees) could each appoint three members to the state committee. Incumbents and nonincumbent nominees had the same appointing power. Given the law, it seemed to us that the Republican Party of California was destined to be taken over by the crazies and their ability to out-vote incumbents.

But Phil offered to help. Assemblyman Tom Bane had a bill to amend the government code affecting the Democratic Party. Phil asked Bane to amend this bill to provide Republican incumbents with nine appointments (rather than three) to the Republican State Committee and he further said, "I'll get the Governor (Pat Brown) to sign it." The bill was amended at Phil's request, and in its amended form went to the governor for signature. But Pat Brown was opposed to the original Democratic Party provision, and informed Phil that the bill would be vetoed.

A stirring arose within Phil—he had promised me and other Republican incumbents that the governor would sign the bill. To keep his promise, he then demanded that Pat Brown sign half a bill! And that is what happened. Though it is absolutely unauthorized by statute (governors sign bills, they can't amend them), Phil Burton prevailed on Governor Brown to veto half a bill and to sign the other half! Thus half a bill was sent to the secretary of state for final enrollment in state statutes.

In a typical "days work" fashion, Phil Burton had kept his word (a commentary on Phil's integrity) and, without challenge, the statute governing the membership makeup of the Republican State Central Committee went into effect. Thereafter, the Republican State Committee was dominated by incumbents and their appointees. Relatively rational officers were elected in 1966, sound resolutions were passed, and the kooks were contained. Political tranquility prevailed.

It is thus that the California Republican Party was saved from destructive and disastrous far-right, neo-fascist domination, for a while. And, not by coincidence, the Ronald Reagan forces began to rise from the ashes of 1964—but without the Birch taint that had helped bury the Goldwater effort in California. The party and the Reagan for governor campaign could now claim to be constructively conservative. Reagan, too, shunned the crazies who now could not dominate the state party machinery.

Ronald Reagan, of course, was elected governor of California in 1966. Phil Burton had left the Assembly for his new congressional seat. But Ronald and Phil were to meet again, in Washington. Though all of the above is factually reported and did occur, I cannot state that, years later, Ronald Reagan thanked Phil Burton for helping create a Republican atmosphere that allowed candidate Reagan to become the governor of California and then president of the United States. But in the context of the above, it is clear that Phil Burton deserves that credit!

2. University Funding

(Editor's note: This piece was originally written in response to an article by Ward Connerly, also a former regent, which discussed the "spiraling costs of higher education" and blamed them partly on a UC administration that operates with a lack of fiscal oversight.)

Ward Connerly criticizes UC administrators but misses the major point and cause of spiraling costs—the abdication of state governments over the last 50 years. In the early 1950s there was no tuition at our colleges and universities. At UC the "incidental fee"—health care, etc.—was $65 per year. Room and board could be had for $100 per month. UC's tuition is now $6,500+ (up to $8,000 since this was written and some graduate schools much higher) and room and board is $1,000+ per month. Do the arithmetic: inflation over the last 50 years has been about 1,000% (i.e., gasoline was 30¢, a quart of milk was 15¢) but the cost of entering the UC system has increased 10,000%. Visualize that on a graph.

Another fact: In the legislature's Golden Years (1960s), 60% of UC's annual operating budget was supported by the state's General Fund; now it is less than 30%. There are at least two reasons for this 100% decrease: (1) ballot box budgeting initiatives have allocated and thus frozen more and more of remaining discretionary state dollars; (2) legislative abdication—it is much more politic to place the increased tuition burden on the middle-class family (the regents of course vote the higher fees), rather than raise tax money to pay for what was virtually a free education years ago.

I paid $60 per year for three years at UC's Boalt Hall Law School. That would cost $75,000 today! Fortunately UC's administrators have fashioned a combination of student loans and financial aid (paid for by the higher tuition) to relieve some students of some of the above burden. Credit goes to UC's administrators.

Connerly's commentary blames administrative salaries and "inefficiencies" for the spiraling costs. We can stipulate that efficiencies are needed, but the percentage effect of administrator salaries on a $12 billion dollar operating budget for 150,000 plus UC students is almost zero.

Lastly, the complaining Connerly would have us believe that "a structure that insulates (the university) from outside influences" is not desirable.

Again, the facts: the university was constitutionally created and thus insulated so that political causes and forces cannot (or should not) affect university operations. One example of the perversion of this process is former Gov. Pete Wilson running for president in 1995, rabidly supporting Connerly's sponsorship of Prop. 209, which caused the board of regents by a 14-to-10 vote to ban all attempts to foster diversity at the university. Connerly led the effort at the board. The ultimate irony to all of this is that UC's president and campus chancellors, of whom Connerly now complains, all opposed his action.

Connerly, in the meantime, was profiting measurably from fees and commissions derived from contributions supporting his sponsorship of comparable initiatives in a host of other states.

Note this significant excerpt from a speech delivered by Gen. Colin Powell to the Republican National Convention in 2000:

> We must understand, my friends, we must understand that there is a problem out there for us. We must understand the cynicism that exists in the black community, the kind of cynicism that is created when, for example, some in our Party miss no opportunity to roundly and loudly condemn 'Affirmative Action' that has helped a few thousand black kids get an education . . . . We must understand, my friends.

Every 25 years or so the board of regents, influenced by outside political influences, causes harm to the university and its reputation: loyalty oaths in the '50s, Governor Reagan's firing of President Clark Kerr in the late '60's, and the Connerly/Wilson political move to support Prop. 209 in 1995.

Unrelated but interesting, President Kerr writes of three major diversions from academic administration: parking for the faculty, athletics for the alumni, and sex for the students. I believe that social change has solved one of those problem areas.

My view: members of the University Board of Regents have two primary duties—to give continuing sage advice to the university's officers who are engaged to run this world-renowned institution and to do no harm. Regental appointments are stated to be prestigious positions—but it is not they who are prestigious, it is the university!

Governors rarely, very rarely, attend UC regents meetings, but just-elected Ronald Reagan on January 22, 1967, led a vote to fire nationally renowned President Clark Kerr. Ten days before, at a Sutter Club UC reception for legislators, attending regents convened a rump meeting (illegal after my 1970 constitutional amendment) to discuss that forthcoming action. I had informed President Kerr of the meeting.

This of course was a blow to the university—a rehash of the 1964–1965 Free Speech Movement and its offshoot, the so-called Filthy Speech Movement. Many "innovative" placards proclaimed: **F**reedom **U**nder **C**lark **K**err, with exaggerated first letters.

More on Ballot Box Budgeting

Legislators, in the term-limited era of no long-term thinking, default in their duties. They gradually allow massive fee and tuition increases to replace the hard task of supplying state budget money to the University. Though low-income students benefit from grants and University fee subsidies, middle-class parents are being creamed. Yet the legislature and governors find it easier to have UC regents continually raise tuition, a massively progressive selective tax on income. That is the existing state policy of partial privatization of the university, on the backs of parents.

For perspective, go back 50 years. There was no tuition at UC—I paid a $60 "incidental" fee, graduating in 1949. By the 1950s fees ran about $75.00 per year. Tuition today is near $8,500, a 10,000+% increase in 50 years compared to an inflation rate of 1,000%. Recall if you can that gasoline was in the 40-cents-per-gallon range, postage was 5 cents, bridge fare 50 cents—all today experiencing a near 1,000% increase .

Why this dramatic disparity? Blame ballot box budgeting, Proposition 13, Proposition 98 (K-12 funding), and others. Governmental processes and physics are similar—vacuums attract. In 1978, Prop. 13 severely limited local government's ability to fund then local obligations. That vacuum was filled by the state assuming the financing, and the power, over all health and welfare costs, even the whole local court system. Throughout succeeding decades, voters drained virtually every remaining discretionary state budget dollar, resulting in only about a three billion dollar state "contribution" to a 12 billion dollar UC regular operating annual budget. Likewise over the last 30 years, there has been an increasing multitude of local and state fee increases replacing more broadly based taxation.

Over the years, the university has been a great economic engine for our state. But we are well on our way to doing the university and the state permanent harm unless all of us respond.

The initial decline of the state support for the University of California started and continued for 16 years with the advent of Governors Ronald Reagan and Jerry Brown (1967–1982). Reagan clamped down on the UC system reacting to the earlier 1960s Free Speech Movement (i.e., riots); and Jerry Brown thought UC to be "elitist," part of his "small is beautiful" effort to change California's culture. Even in the face of Proposition 13's budgetary impact (post 1978), Gov. George Deukmejian, during UC President David Gardner's administration, significantly increased state support. That did not last; massive tuition increases occurred from 1990 until the present day.

The Board of Regents

Let us add a comment or two regarding governance of the university by the board of regents over the last 60 years. Proposition 209 barring any state-supported "affirmative action" was dying at the signature-gathering stage without concerted monetary and political support until Governor Wilson and his former 1969 legislative committee consultant, Regent Ward Connerly, teamed up in 1995 to use the University of California as their tool to propound their political cause.

Wilson was running for president in the Republican primary and personally, pointedly lobbied the board of regents to vote to ban affirmative action—which then breathed life into the 209 campaign. Connerly carried the day with Wilson literally presiding at the board and conducting, at the board, nationally televised "debates" with Jesse Jackson—good politics in a Republican primary! The result was (1) a dramatic reduction of minority enrollment, particularly black students who, though totally qualified, boycotted UC—refusing even to apply; this was corrected seven years later when the board (with a lot of background work by President Atkinson and this author) rescinded the 1995 resolution—but Prop. 209 had already passed (53% to 47%) and thus controlled; and (2) Connerly went into the ballot business, making major money promoting similar measures in a number of other states.

Prior to 1970, the regents, constitutionally constituted and mostly immune from state statutes, conducted their affairs behind closed doors. That changed in 1970 with the passage (by 70%) of Assembly Constitutional Amendment ACA1-Bagley mandating open meetings along with other state bodies.

Over the years, members of the board cannot resist becoming political-promoting causes. And every 25 years or so, the regents do damage to the university. I submit:

1. the despised and unnecessary Loyalty Oath of the early '50s—faculty turmoil resulted;

2. the regents' closed-meeting firing of President Clark Kerr, led by Gov. Ronald Reagan, 1967—totally political;

3. the sponsorship of Proposition 209, by Gov. Pete Wilson trying to be a right-winger in the presidential primary (1995–1996).

The regents, some superb and generally intelligent, but some political appointees have no idea what university governance is all about: they believe that, as stated, their appointment to the board is "the most prestigious" of those made by the governor. No! It is not the board that is prestigious—it is the university .

56

Basically, the board has two main obligations: to appoint the most qualified high-level administration to really run the institution (which generally they/we have done) and to *do no harm!*

3. Arnold Schwarzenegger and Ronald Reagan

Like Ronald Reagan 40 years ago, Arnold Schwarzenegger came to the governor's office with no direct experience in the art of governance. But, like Reagan, he learned. And now, like Reagan, he's received his diploma from the people. They've re-elected him. I believe it is both interesting and ironic to compare the first two years of their respective administrations.

First, Governor Ronald. Parroting an antigovernment speech left over from the disastrous 1964 Barry Goldwater campaign, Governor Reagan came to Sacramento demonizing the town. He had himself sworn-in at 12:01 a.m. to "prevent Pat Brown from looting the Treasury." His declared enemies were "those guys upstairs." His first key appointments were foisted upon him by four Los Angeles multimillionaires—Henry Salvatori, Holmes Tuttle, Justin Dart, and Cy Rubel (the Kitchen Cabinet). It was that group that prevented former San Francisco Assemblyman and Republican Party Chairman Cap Weinberger from being director of finance. Weinberger was "too liberal."

And, of course, Reagan was going to "cut, squeeze, and trim" the budget, plus repeal fair housing, curb the (liberal) University of California, oppose progressive income taxes, etc., etc.

But Governor Reagan recovered from two years of malaise. He fired his first finance director, the one from the Kitchen Cabinet, and appointed Weinberger. And he began to govern. He proposed both tax reform (vastly increasing progressivity to an 11% rate) and welfare reform, both of which we negotiated for months and which I then carried. He began dealing with our then knowledgeable nonterm limited legislators. He signed CEQA, signed the then most liberal abortion bill, endorsed the Equal Rights Amendment, and became a very genuine, decent, likeable leader and governor. What a difference two years made.

And let's not forget "cut, squeeze, and trim": Pat Brown's last budget totaled $4.6 billion dollars; Governor Reagan's budget just four years later had doubled to $10 billion.

Next, Governor Arnold. We need not detail here the present history. We know what happened, pre special election. The state was in significant fiscal trouble—one-time monies had been spent by the Davis folks to expand ongoing programs.

Arnold and Pete Wilson's wranglers came riding to the rescue. Governor Arnold, uninitiated and frankly arrogant, was taken in by key former Wilson staffers who used the new governor to revive and try to pass their old agenda.

For himself, Arnold proclaimed that he was going to collect big monies from Washington. Instead, he has sent about a billion dollars a year back to the IRS by canceling four billion dollars of IRS deductible state taxes and thus increased the state deficit by the same four billion, to boot. He was going to kick butt. We know the rest, now history. The 2008 $16 billion General Fund deficit is the direct result of his $4 billion-a-year tax cut four years ago—i.e., reduction of the vehicle property tax that Gov. Davis had increased. As the *San Francisco Chronicle* wrote (09/10/08), "If Schwarzenegger had not rolled back the vehicle license fee increase, he probably would not have had to propose increasing taxes today."

But happily, Governor Arnold has learned as did Governor Reagan. Though Reagan may have been inspired to really govern by the obvious prospect of the presidency, our now savvy, most cordial, smart, accommodating governor learned because he wanted to succeed, he wanted to govern.

Wisely, he cast aside Wilsonian advisors, brought in new staff, and became Rockefellerian (referring to former New York Gov. Nelson Rockefeller, defeated for the GOP presidential nomination by Goldwater in 1964) in his new approach to consultative, collaborative governing.

God Bless. We have again found the moderate middle of the road. Somehow, as did Ronald, Arnold has contained the far right. But unfortunately the still fractured uncompromisingly partisan legislature, hobbled by term limits, has stymied Governor Arnold's efforts to date.

Sacramento, California
Contact: Lyn Nofziger
445-4571   6.13.67

Governor Ronald Reagan announced today that he will sign a bill liberalizing California's abortion laws, but emphasized that the measure passed by the Legislature falls short of meeting some of his requirements.

"I am fully sympathetic with attempts to liberalize the outdated abortion law now on the law books of California," the governor said in announcing his decision.

"I am confident that the people of California recognize that need and will support the humanitarian goals of the measure as passed by the Assembly and Senate of the State Legislature.

"However, I must be frank and concede that the legislation that will come before me for signature is by no means perfect. There are several areas of concern to me and to many others in California, including members of the Legislature.

"Therefore, I intend to watch very closely the implementation and results of this new legislation and keep a continuing check on how it affects the citizens of this state. And I cannot emphasize too strongly that if any feature of the measure fails to carry out the intent of the Legislature, I will ask for corrective amendments to the law.

"Because of my belief that a liberalization of the abortion laws is necessary, I will sign the bill even though it does not meet each and every objection that I and others in California have to it," the governor said.

Of particular concern to the governor was the lack of a residency clause in the bill.

"We must be extremely careful to assure that this legislation does not result in making California a haven for those who would come to this state solely for the purpose of taking advantage of California's new law," he said.

The governor also said care must be taken to make sure that hospitals are not created for the main purpose of performing abortions.

He reaffirmed his statement made earlier in the day at his weekly press conference that had these requirements been amended into the bill, the legislation would have been improved.

PB/324

60

* <u>Number of Abortions Performed</u>
<u>in California, 1967-74/a</u>

	Total	Financed by Medi-Cal %	Number
1967	518	N/A	N/A
1968	5,018	7.8%	391
1969	15,339	19.5	2,991
1970	65,369	35.8	23,402
1971	116,749	38.5	44,948
1972	138,584	32.1	44,485
1973	131,870/b	32.1	42,330
1974	135,762/b	42.0	57,020
Total	609,209		215,567

/a Source: California Department of Health
/b Does not include abortions performed in private physicians' offices

SUPPLEMENTAL DATA

	Total	Financed by Medi-Cal %	Number
1975 →	142,067	43.2	61,373

Total 759,276 — 4 296,940

12/14/89

— Lucy — Reagan ran for President claiming he had Reformed Welfare (my bill - 1971). But Re Number of MOTHERS on the rolls remained Constant. Only the Children went down. Above numbers show why!!

BH

One area crying for consideration is University of California basic tuition that has increased 10,000% versus the 1,000% inflation rate over the last 50 years, i.e., $60+ per year to $6,500. The state has abdicated, paying for less than 30% of UC's annual operating budget, down from 60% in the 1960–1970 decade!

Addendum: UC tuition has been increased to $8,000-plus in 2008.

12. (previous pages) The press release announcing Gov. Ronald Reagan's 1967 decision to sign a bill liberalizing California abortion laws, along with Bagley's handwriting noting that so-called "welfare savings" were actually caused by fewer children being born. The release was issued by Lyn Nofziger, who was then Reagan's press secretary and later worked in the Reagan White House. Nofziger was the aide who announced that Reagan had been shot by would-be assassin John W. Hinckley, Jr.

4. Ronald Reagan's Real Record

Some commentators want to compare Governor Reagan to the present administration, so let's go back to 1967–1974. Ronald W. Reagan swept the late Governor Pat Brown out of office by a 980,000 vote margin. As is almost always true, it's the incumbent who loses the race. Pat had his problems, although in later years he became known as the man who built California and as one of the best California governors in the 20th century. I agree.

The first two years of the Reagan Administration were near disasters. Initially, Governor Reagan was understandably a rank amateur. He simply believed his own speeches with no means of implementing them. To his credit, however, he did not remain an ideologue. To his credit, he signed our pre-*Roe v. Wade* liberal "choice" bill in 1967, saying that "the people of California . . . will support the humanitarian goals of the measure." Later he stated that he was "in full support of the Equal Rights Amendment and will be pleased if you are able to find a use for my name in attracting additional support," writing to the E.R.A. group. Folks don't recall these facts.

And though his 1966 campaign speeches accused Governor Brown of "looting" the treasury and the candidate claimed that he would "cut, trim, and squeeze" the budget—Pat Brown's last budget of $4.6 billion grew in Gov. Reagan's first four years to $10 billion.

Ronald Reagan was a very pleasant man; legislators loved to talk with him, listen to his stories and jokes. But in the earlier years, he blamed and castigated "those guys upstairs."

It is to the eternal credit of the new Republican Speaker at the time (by just 41 votes), Bob Monagan, that in January 1969 Bob broached the governor and said, in effect, "Let's start governing." Also, the governor's newer replacement staff (Weinberger became director of finance) awakened to the fact that he could/should run for president.

From that point, Reagan began personally negotiating tax reform and welfare reform—meeting with a set bipartisan group for multiple weeks on end. I had been the chairman of "revenue and taxation" with Monagan and then of the "welfare" committee in 1971 appointed by new Democratic Speaker Bob Moretti, and became the moderate middle man in these negotiations, over a period of four years.

The tax bills (AB 1000, 1001, Bagley, which became SB90) added the 9, 10, and 11% income tax rates and narrowed the brackets. That narrowing caused the huge bracket-jump during the later (Pres. Jimmy Carter) inflation, giving Jerry Brown a $6 billion surplus and literally causing the passage of Prop. 13. We should have indexed the brackets. I claim the blame.

We also raised the corporate tax rate but reduced some property taxes and ultimately repealed the business inventory tax. That was the trade-off, but the fact remains that we raised the state tax take by $2 billion—a 20% increase in a $10 billion budget.

Welfare reform was a little different. Ronald Reagan did some demagoguery, fanning the flames, but we finally negotiated a bill with John Burton, Leo McCarthy, Bob Moretti, with me and Ronald Reagan in agreement. It took two months with Reagan's Chief of Staff Ed Meese and the governor in almost daily meetings, in 1972, including Senators Tony Beilenson and Clair Burgener.

The Bagley-Beilenson Bill was signed, and the governor later claimed a $2 billion savings when running for president in 1976 (against my friend, then President Jerry Ford). Some have concluded that this challenge to President Ford caused the Carter victory.

But the legislative analyst then, totally respected A. Alan Post (whom Reagan called Alan A. Post), testified in 1975 that the real savings were only $50 million. There were additional savings, though not from the welfare bill.

The unheralded fact is that under the 1972 Welfare Act the number of eligible mothers on Aid to Families with Dependent Children remained the same. But the number of children on "welfare" was reduced by close to 300,000 (1967 to 1975). That was the almost exact number of now le-

State of California
GOVERNOR'S OFFICE
SACRAMENTO 95814

January 13, 1972.

Mrs. Barbara Trister
President, Theta Sigma Phi
819 Santee Street, Room 411
Los Angeles, California 90014

Dear Mrs. Trister:

I appreciate very much your invitation to the
Getting to Know the Amendment Meeting on
January 21. I sincerely regret not being
able to attend.

However, I am in full support of the Equal
Rights Amendment and will be pleased if you
are able to find a use for my name in attracting
additional support.

While I will not have time to be with you, please
extend my best wishes and hopes for success to
all those present.

Sincerely,

RONALD REAGAN
Governor

13. *(previous page) A letter from Gov. Ronald Reagan vowing his "full support" of the proposed Equal Rights Amendment to the U.S. Constitution, which eventually died when it was not ratified by enough state legislatures. Conservatives strongly opposed this women's rights amendment.*

14. *(above) At a tax reform press conference in the state Capitol, (left to right), Sen. Robert Lagomarsino, Gov. Ronald Reagan, Bagley, and Assembly Speaker Robert T. Monagan.*

gal abortions financed by Medi-Cal (Dept. of Health Statistics). Thus the welfare costs were drastically reduced by our "choice" bill of 1967, happily signed by Gov. Reagan and *not* by so-called welfare reform. Welfare eligibility had not been affected.

Ronald Reagan was an effective governor once he abandoned his 1966 campaign speeches and agreed to negotiate substantive solutions in a bipartisan way. He did very well, always pleasant, never arrogant. But one mark of the ideologue remained. He continued to demand the repeal of the 1963 Fair Housing Law authored by former Assemblyman Byron Rumford, as he had in the 1966 campaign.

Outright repeal, SBI, passed the Senate in 1967 and was sent purposefully by then Speaker Jesse Unruh to the Assembly Judiciary Committee, of which I was chairman. We then fashioned compromise amendments and the Senate nonconcurred as expected. A conference committee was appointed late in the session; As chairman, I simply never convened the committee; fair housing remains the law. Anyone wish to repeal fair housing legislation today?

5. Initiatives

Herewith is a short thesis on how three initiatives (Prop. 9, political reform of 1974; Prop. 13, property tax reform of 1978; and Prop. 140, term limits of 1990) have seriously affected the ability to govern in California.

Jerry Brown's Prop. 9 was ballot leverage for his governor's race against State Controller Hugh Flournoy. Prop. 9 passed and Jerry won by 90,000 votes, but bipartisan collegiality was destined to be destroyed. By limiting lobbyist gifts to legislators at $10 per month, the Political Reform Act ended lobbyist-sponsored bipartisan dinners, lunches, and gatherings that had allowed members to mingle and get to know each other and develop friendship and trust. These pleasant gatherings costing less than $20 per legislator were replaced by $3,000-plus, one-party fundraisers, hundreds of them in some months.

The bipartisan gatherings didn't disappear at once. In fact, the best known lunch group, the California Derby Club, continued until 1997 before being done in by both Prop. 9 and by Prop. 140's term limits.

"Derby" continued in part because it was a membership group, and the legislators who ran it restricted the number of legislators who could belong. Consequently, the lobbyist members of "Derby" always outnumbered its legislative members. This fact, along with careful bookkeeping, which included charging the whole bar tab to the lobbyists, allowed Derby's lobby members to continue paying for legislator lunches without violating the Prop. 9 limit. If there were an overage, the extra amount was billed to the legislators.

But other such gatherings, like "Moose Milk," were not membership groups. We sometimes had 50 or 60 legislators showing up for a free lunch every Thursday during sessions—Assemblymen/women and senators, Democrats and Republicans gathered together. And since there was no way three or four host lobbyists could comply with the $10 limit, those gatherings disappeared.

Prop. 9 also had an effect on campaign finance. Pre Prop. 9, the normal campaign contribution was about $200 in the Assembly. The California

State Employees Association and Superior Oil were good for $500 each. (Superior Oil lobbyist Monroe Butler gave his $500 in cash.) As a result, there were no fundraisers in Sacramento pre 1974. The system was cut-and-dried. Everybody knew the regular, limited amount that was always forthcoming. Nobody had to call every lobbyist under the sun to raise a few bucks. (This didn't apply to the Speaker and a few senators who had their own funding sources.)

There were always exceptions. A major bill (i.e., Governor Reagan's $2 billion state tax increase on a $10 billion budget, which I carried in 1969–70) provoked one sleazy senator to withhold his needed 26th or 27th vote and ask for $10,000 and also have his law partner appointed a judge. I believe he received a $10,000 contribution from a lobbyist who was trying to help.

Because lobby contributions to legislative candidates were basically limited by the lobbyists' known budgets, total campaign costs were likewise, the maximum being $30,000–$40,000 per campaign year. But if members had no opposition, they could pocket this money.

Thus Speaker Jesse Unruh would tell Democratic Party leaders not to run a candidate against (for example) Santa Barbara Republican Jim Holmes, who then of course was "indebted" to Jesse because Holmes could pocket the money.

(In 1963 Unruh urged his "indebted" Republicans to support Charlie Conrad in Conrad's campaign to become Republican Floor Leader, giving Conrad the winning edge. Jesse could then operate without major minority opposition.)

Others played the "no-opposition" game. State Democratic Chairman Roger Kent of Kentfield, hoping to create an open seat in his Marin County Assembly district, promised Marin-Sonoma Republican Assemblyman Dick McCollister a free ride in 1958 if McCollister would not run again in 1960. McCollister agreed, thus profiting in 1958. But the open seat failed to go Democratic. It's the one I won in 1960.

All of this was then possible because of the very lax reporting requirements: (1) You could keep left-over campaign contributions (paying income tax, I suppose); (2) there was no reporting requirement for contributors, thus no cross-checking; (3) members reported very selectively, one example being to report the name of the bank cashier on a cashier check donation; and (4) there was no real break-down of campaign expenditures.

But all of this laxity could have been stopped by simply requiring reciprocal reporting, matching contributors' names and amounts (under oath) with candidate receipts—instead of the draconian Prop. 9. By preventing lobbyists from contributing and even making recommendations (the latter ultimately declared unconstitutional) this political reform caused the proliferation of special interest PACs that in turn brought about the massive onslaught of fundraisers asking for multiple thousands instead of the former limited $200 average. Beware: politics and physics are similar, vacuums attract. Further, the explosive growth of the disguised and despised "Independent Expenditure Committee" hit pieces, separately funded, is directly attributable to the dollar limitation of direct campaign contributions.

Because Prop. 13 and term limits are of more recent vintage, less need be said. But the deterioration of trust and collegiality continued. With the passage of Proposition 13 came a whole allied group of so-called "Prop. 13 babies," young Republicans who demanded less government but more partisanship. They demanded to be able to sit together on the Assembly Floor, thus ending a century of bipartisan seating. For the first time, party aisles were instituted. And since collegial lunches and dinners no longer took place, members' knowledge of and trust in each other also further dissolved.

Prop. 13 also had the undesirable (and liberal) effect of concentrating power and money in Sacramento, thus converting local Home Rule to a homey homily.

And then we have Term Limits. It does take about three or four years to get to know and understand your colleagues, to learn whom you can trust and to learn enough about a $100 billion enterprise to be able to function and possibly have an effect. Now after four years (in the Assembly) you are a lame duck, and two-thirds of your colleagues are gone. Thus there is little effort to establish long-term trust, to collaborate in order to develop relationships that lead to leadership ad policy development and changes. And so, lo and behold, Freshmen become Speakers and Minority Leaders, with absolutely no background knowledge.

Collegiality has been consigned to the ash can, partisan ideology has been unleashed, campaign contributions and therefore expenditures have expanded far above the rate of inflation, and the art of compromise and thus governance has been eroded.

Beware of initiatives and ideologues—if the voting public would only know. Did they know that Howard Jarvis, a garrulous and rather profane right-winger (whom I debated) was president of the Apartment House Owners Association whose aim was to freeze property taxes on commercial property? Did voters know that ex-legislator Pete Shabarum sponsored term limits to get even with his "colleagues" who had mistreated him? Again, I debated him; he won, he got even.

6. Fundraisers: Dollars Instead of Dinners!

On one of the last days of the 2005 session, there were 18 announced fundraisers where one guest could have spent a total of $43,000 for the evening. That plethora of PAC money was spawned by Proposition 9, Jerry Brown's "political reform" initiative of 1974. Prior to Prop. 9, there were no PACs. There were *no* fund-raising events in Sacramento, none. And incidentally, there were no "aisles" separating legislators by party. Democrat Al Alquist called me "seatmate" for years, until his death at the age of 90.

So why no fundraisers? Because we all knew the budgets of all lobbyists, i.e., Hal Broaders of the Bank of America was good for $200 every two years; CSEA had a $500 per member limit (possibly double for senators). Thus there were no fundraisers because we all knew of the finite amount available, like clockwork, every two years.

Importantly, the total amount of all such contributions ranged between $20,000 and $40,000 per Assembly race; thus that became the total cost of the average campaign, plus some local money.

PACs did not exist. But when Prop. 9 outlawed lobbyist contributions, PACs (filling the vacuum) sprung up. They were based out of town, impersonal, and had no known limit. So have a $3,600 fundraiser the night before the bank bill!

These have replaced ongoing lobby-hosted collegial lunches and dinners for members at a then cost of about $20 each. Prop. 9 limited lobbyist spending to $10 per month per member. In Jerry's words "Two hamburgers and a coke," once a month.

So friendship, understanding, and thus consensus government slowly disappeared because of "political reform." Ideology then trumped collegiality.

7. Every Night Is Saturday Night

The very perceptive Dan Walters writing in the *Sacramento Bee* recently observed: The legislature has "shunned engagement with the issues that arise out of California's growth and social and economic change, made huge mistakes when it deigned to do anything (energy and budget . . .), wasted its time and our money on trivial [bills], and in general abdicated its responsibilities."

Why is this so when in 1969–70 the California Legislature was named number one in the nation? That is when nonideologue moderates—both parties—controlled a mostly collegial body. There were no "aisles." Folks served long enough to develop friendship and trust, mutual respect, and subject matter expertise. We passed leading-edge legislation in many fields that is on the books of today—health, welfare, local government, water, environment, civil rights, law enforcement, educational equalization, and supportive revenue measures.

You can blame term limits but let's start with the rise of ideology and the demise of collegiality. Why do we now suffer from this hardening of the categories? Here are the facts from our Golden Years.

In the words of then Senator Frank Peterson (D-Fort Bragg), "Every night is Saturday Night." Prior to the 1974 Jerry Brown Proposition 9, lunches and dinners were always bipartisan, hosted by lobbyists.

Prior to 1967, sessions were constitutionally limited to 180 legislative days every other year, with an intervening one-month budget session in March. From 1967 forward, annual sessions lasted about six months. Part-time legislators went home, practiced law, sold insurance, ran their businesses or farms. They raised funds and lived in their districts and traveled the state on interim committees. There were always hosted lunches and dinners for the committee and staff, all over the state. We learned geography together.

Lobbyists had their part-time offices in the then Senator and El Mirador (now an old folks' home) hotels. Always bipartisan dinners (and card games) were hosted in these hotel suites. Then there was the California

Derby Club (C.D.C.), the Tuesday lunch. And there was an all-hands open house lunch on Thursdays at the Top of the El Mirador, named "Moose Milk" by Senator John Begovich (D-Jackson). Great food, good drinks, total collegiality, and the lobby costs were a pittance compared to today's obscene nightly, all-partisan fundraisers. Beware of misdirected reform.

Ways and Means Chairman and later Vice Chairman Frank Lanterman (R-La Canada) would sit at his favorite table in the Senator dining room. Folks came by to visit. And we had dinners at The Firehouse, at Fat's, then we "adjourned" to the Torch Club just down from Fat's. Senator Henry Mello (D-Watsonville) played the piano. Speaker Jesse Unruh sang country songs.

Every Monday night there was an organized poker game in the El Mirador Penthouse suite (occupied during the day by Kent Redwine, movie lobbyist, and then by Danny Creeden, beer lobbyist.) Players were Speaker Bob Monagan (R-Tracy), later Speaker Bob Moretti (D-No. Hollywood), Frank Murphy (R-Santa Cruz), later Speaker Willie Brown (D-San Francisco), myself, and other Democrats and Republicans. The leadership of both parties in the Assembly played poker together for years, at night. We did not cheap shot each other during the day.

At times the games lasted almost all night. So, when in 1971 Willie Brown became chairman (he was a chairman and we were assemblymen and women) of Ways and Means, which then met on Tuesday mornings, we did not change the card game—we changed Ways and Means to Wednesdays! Appropriations still meets on Wednesdays, and that is why.

This bipartisan collegiality prevailed until the 1974 Proposition 9 cutoff lobby hosting, and then Prop. 13 (1978) brought us the Jarvis Republican ideologues who insisted for the first time in history that the Assembly sit in partisan aisles. Gone were the dinner and overnight bipartisan train trips to Reno casinos and back, by tagging a private car onto Southern Pacific trains returning in time for roll call. Since one can lose his or her office by accepting free rides from a railroad, that problem was solved by lobbyist Al Schultz and others simply buying the train tickets. S.P. provided the dinners.

In those legislative hey-days committee roll calls were rarely demanded, voice votes were called by the trusted chairman or woman; there were no caucus staff-prepared vote sheets (now written by staff kids); members had one administrative assistant (after 1966) and one secretary. Other than long-time committee staff, there were no chiefs of staff, no legislative directors, and no Capitol directors. We did have committee analyses and, Good Gaw'd, we sometimes actually read the bills, and without caucus staff guidance we decided how to vote! We solved the problems of the then 20 million Californians.

8. Ideologues and Then Moderates

Beware of ideologues—they lose. In that context let's review a little history of the wing movements within the parties. This is now most relevant because of the recent right-wing comments about the Susan Kennedy appointment as Schwarzenegger's chief of staff.

Think of Goldwater's massive loss to Johnson (by 1.9 million in California) and then McGovern who won only one state against Nixon in 1972. Ideologues lose.

Go back to 1958 when U.S. Senator Bill Knowland pulled the financial rug from under Governor Goodwin Knight so that he (Knowland) could run for governor on a right-to-work platform. Knowland lost to Attorney General Pat Brown by a 20-point margin, and the Assembly went from a former 50–30 Republican majority to a later 45–35 Democratic margin. Earlier, the 1961 reappointment led to a later Republican nadir of 27 in the Assembly and 13 in the Senate.

Then came the rise of the John Birch Society. In heavily democratic districts where no Republican in his or her right mind would run, Birch members ran and tried to take over party machinery, i.e., nonincumbent nominees would outnumber incumbents by a two-to-one margin. The result was no Republican Party Platform in 1964.

At about 6:00 p.m. when the sane folks left for a drink and dinner, the majority nonincumbent nominees had a platform plank on the floor, ready for a vote, "To Send the Blacks Back to Africa."

Yes, that happened, and the horrible plank could have passed. Happily "we" still had the chair. Congressman Bill Maillard (R-San Francisco) was presiding. We called for a quorum and Maillard instantly adjourned the Platform Convention without a platform. Shame on the right-wing.

This was also the era of extreme exercise of power by Speaker Jesse Unruh, made possible by the paucity of opposition and some just plain sell-outs. First, Unruh engineered the creation of the then unneeded and unrequested 5th District Court of Appeal in Fresno so that Speaker Ralph

Brown could be appointed justice. Then with himself as the new Speaker, he literally had Charlie Conrad elected minority leader. Jesse owned many Republican members. He assured them no Democratic opposition (they pocketed their contributions).

He would send friendly Republicans to Washington, D.C., at 15-cents per mile. That's $900 in your pocket when the airfare was about $200. Recall that the legislative "salary" was then $500 per month. Interim committee assignments added per diems and even some very personal "needs" were provided by the Speaker to selected supportive friends.

Jesse was a master. He provided the swing votes in the Republican Caucus to elect Conrad! Again, this was made possible by the earlier losses caused by Republican right-wing ideologues.

The overnight lockup (with Army cots in the chamber) of Republican members in 1963 will be the subject of a future item. In the mid and late sixties, the moderates—Bob Monagan, Jack Veneman, Hugh Flournoy, Gordon Cologne, myself, and then George Deukmejian, Pete Wilson, Bob Beverly, Ken Maddy, Gordon Duffy, Gene Chappie, Jerry Lewis, Bill Campbell, Frank Murphy, Vic Veysey, Dixon Arnett, Paul Priolo, et al.— recovered the majority and in 1969 we elected Bob Monagan Speaker with 41 votes, and Howard Way became Senate President Pro-Tem.

When you have a balanced House, 42–38 Democratic in 1967 and 41–39 Republican in 1969, everybody has a voice with resultant good government. With a political balance returned, Jesse Unruh's power was curtailed, and he became a statesman. Much leading-edge legislation was passed and California's Legislature was named number one in the nation. We had learned to govern.

At the same time, Jesse Unruh fought the very left-leaning California Democratic Council and prevailed against the ideologues who would have moved the Democratic Party far to the left. These were California's Golden Years of growth and good governance.

9. Redistricting

Giving or receiving consideration for a deal in exchange for a vote is a felony. Money is only one form of payment; direct political barter is another. In my legislative service I witnessed many a bipartisan felony committed during passage of reapportionment bills, 1961, 1966, 1971 (vetoed) and 1973.

A Democratic Speaker of the Assembly would provide a specific safe district for a Republican member in exchange for an ongoing pledge to cast key votes, many internal and procedural, as the Speaker wished. (Be assured the same would have been true if the political parties were reversed.)

Also, the affected Republican legislator might be promised that he or she would not face a funded candidate from the opposition party in November. (Prior to the passage of Prop. 9 in 1974, some members would personally pocket the now unnecessary and unexpended campaign money.)

Equally, of course, a member who refused the proposed sellout could be punished by an unfavorable alteration of his or her district lines, or even total elimination of the district, but that is just one-sided retribution, not a felony.

Gov. Ronald Reagan was so appalled by this legislative legerdemain that he vetoed the 1971 reapportionment bill. Later, in order for an election to proceed, the California Supreme Court appointed a neutral panel of masters (retired judges) to redraw the lines, with resultant districts untainted with either deals or extreme partisanship. For a while we actually had some meaningful contested November general elections.

More recently, and dramatized by the 2001–2002 reapportionment, leaders of both parties cut themselves a joint deal freezing or fixing elections for the ensuing 10 years so that there would be no real contests in November. It is stated that White House operatives urged this cooperation, thus to be assured of no loss of California Republican congressional seats.

Everybody's seat was vested by creating districts where the opposing party had absolutely no realistic chance of victory short of extreme malfeasance by the incumbent. The cynical facts of political life show that this prevented either party from gaining or losing more than a seat or two to date over the whole 2000 decade, out of hundreds of district elections.

These party-heavy districts led to many seats occupied by either far-right Republican or far-left Democratic Party nominees. The automatic November election of these party ideologues can, with few exceptions, lead to the near elimination of the art of compromise. Until the advent of Gov. Arnold Schwarzenegger, "moderates" were a nearly extinct species in California. Government had to take a backseat to partisan ideological gridlock.

There is a double irony here: Senate districts are also partisan extremist-oriented, and now with term limits a member of the Assembly knows when "his or her" Senate seat-to-be will be open. Thus even the moderate member must vote strict hard line or risk defeat in the upcoming Senate primary.

But Governor Arnold will not be governor in 2011, the year of the next required decennial redistricting when ultra-partisan passions and resulting gridlock could again prevail. Legislators could again cut themselves their own piece of legislative district pie, thus depriving others of even a possible taste of victory.

Legislators were devising a scheme to modify this process but did not want to give up ultimate control of "their" boundary lines. Under the legislature's plan, congressional district lines would be exempted from any reform because the state's congressional delegation would oppose. House Speaker Nancy Pelosi states that Congress should control state congressional districts nationwide—pure sophistry. That will never happen.

There is one present solution—a ballot proposition requiring fair, nonpartisan redistricting.

Post-script:

Voters, after years of prior initiative attempts, have finally passed a measure—Proposition 11 in November 2008—to reform redistricting. Incumbents and party forces will no longer be in total control of their "owned" district lines. Gov. Arnold Schwarzenegger, frustrated by partisan gridlock, gets minor credit for this very close victory. Some argue that lobbyists and strong interest groups are also responsible for extreme partisanship but, beyond party leaders, there are ongoing causes of the present abject failure of California's legislative process going back 50 years.

Though new fair election districts will bring us some actual contestable elections and thus will be a moderating force, all will not be cordial collegiality leading to trust, cooperation, compromise. In the course of the last century we have eliminated "cross filing" (a 1914 Hiram Johnson effort that decreased party power), repealed in 1959 by the then new Democratic majority. We next eliminated the basis of members' trust and confidence in each other—Propositions 9 and 13 as discussed. Then in 1990 the term limit initiative placed a final nail in any possibility of long-term friendships and trust. And in 2004, we defeated the remaining proposed solution, the open primary.

The Open Primary

Another solution to soften the extremist ideologues in either party is the open primary, which would allow all registered voters, including those who decline to state, to vote for legislative offices in either (any) party primary. This benefits the more moderate candidate, Democrat or Republican, who can appeal to this broader spectrum of voters—counteracting the far left or far right. A small band of us, with Governor Arnold's help, raised $2 million in 2004 to place this process on the ballot. But the legislature, both parties conspiring, placed a deceptive competing measure on the same ballot and thus defeated the open primary. Again the extremists prevailed.

But the 2010 ballot will again give voters the opportunity to adopt the open primary.

10. What Happened to Moderation and Compromise? A Summary of Many Earlier Comments

Why is there abject failure of the legislative process in Sacramento? What has happened to moderation and compromise?

In 1966, Gov. Pat Brown's last budget was $4.6 billion. We Republican legislators would object, knock off $200 million, claim victory and vote "aye." The two-thirds majority vote needed to pass a budget was overcome.

We were there to govern.

Four years later, Gov. Ronald Reagan's budget was $10 billion. I negotiated and authored the governor's $2 billion tax hike.

We were there to govern.

Trust and longtime friendships trumped ideologies and thus provided the legislative glue. There were no partisan aisles in the chamber. We sat together, ate together, and played together .

But by 2000, partisan self-interest was so rampant that members simply vested their seats, heavily right and heavily left, and left no seats realistically contestable and left no room for moderation.

There is little substantive debate over the need to revise the present self-serving protective method of drawing legislative districts, as now approved by the recent Proposition 11. That will, to some extent, help end partisan stagnation and gridlock in Sacramento after 2012 and the new census.

But the real and ongoing cause of the present abject failure of California's legislative process is 50 years of living political history, from 1959 to the present, as follows:

• Cross filing: The ability to run in the other party primary was adopted in 1914 as one of Gov. Hiram Johnson's reforms, but repealed in 1959 by a newly elected Democratic majority.

• So-called political reform: The Proposition 9 initiative sponsored by then gubernatorial candidate Jerry Brown was passed in 1974. The political cry to eliminate lobby wining and dining did just that. No more bipartisan lunches and dinners because of a $10-per-month limit on lobbyist-hosted meals. Over time, members no longer knew each other, no longer learned to trust and work with each other. Collegiality was killed. Lobbying, of course, continued with massive partisan $3,000-per-ticket contribution events, instead of buying a $25 bipartisan dinner.

• Proposition 13 in 1978: The tax-limiting initiative brought a new cadre of conservative Republican members who demanded partisan aisles in the Assembly. Theretofore, Democrats and Republicans sat together, enjoyed bipartisan friendships, and worked together.

The same post-Proposition 13 partisanship led to separate party caucus positions on all bills—usually staff-written positions followed by members. The message: "Don't read the bill, just vote as told." So sad.

• The 1990 term limit initiative placed a final nail in any remaining collegial bipartisanship and moderation. One-third of the Assembly membership is replaced every two years; two thirds in four years.

Any semblance of long-term reciprocal trust and friendship is going. New members seemingly just fall in line and vote by rote.

The ultimate irony of term limits is that you know when the next state Senate vacancy will occur and as an assemblyman or woman you vote straight party, hard right or hard left, to assure yourself of the upcoming Senate nomination.

This symptom feeds upon itself and prevents present and even future compromises. Gridlock is guaranteed now because the Assembly and Senate districts are all drawn to concentrate the seats together in single-party-dominated enclaves. Compromise has become a dirty word.

Open primaries would allow all voters, including the vast number of decline-to-state registrants, to pick any party primary ballot and vote for its legislative and congressional candidates. By simple arithmetic that system would dilute the voice of party extremists.

Now, as extreme ideological gridlock continues, it becomes more necessary to again propose open primary reform and, with legislative action stalemated, it becomes more and more likely to succeed.

(This piece originally appeared in the *Marin Independent-Journal*, and is reprinted with permission.)

11. Infrastructure—No Longer Golden

Ah, infrastructure. What a wonderful word implying the need for continuing capital investment in transportation, water, education, public safety-building for California's future. Now let's put that in perspective.

"California" was the name of a mythical paradise on earth created by the Spanish writer Montalvo in his *Las Sergas de Esplandian* romance novel, a paradise endowed by "gold, pearls, and beautiful black amazons." This fanciful place name was applied to early maps of Mexico's and (now) our Pacific Coast by some unknown but literate Spanish explorer in the mid-1500s. One wonders whether paradise will become purgatory in the 21st century. Paradise lost?—from Siskiyou to San Diego and from Mono to Monterey!

Other than transit and freeway expansion, the only major state capital construction during the last few decades has been prisons! Consider these numbing numbers: inflation for the last 50 years calculates out at about 1,000%, including gasoline from 40¢ to $4.00, postage stamps from 4¢ to now over 40 cents. But UC tuition has increased from a flat $60 per year (1949 when I entered Boalt Hall) to today's $8,000-plus. State budget support has dropped from 60% of UC's operating budget in the '60s to less than 30%. That is just plain abdication by state government, inspired by "small is beautiful" Jerry Brown following cuts by Ronald Reagan. George Deukmejian did try to reverse this course after a 16-year drought.

California's last major waterway was funded by a 1960 $1.75 billion bond issue; the last bay crossing construction was the Coronado Bridge. But these good works continue to serve us to this day. For historical perspective note that the Golden Gate Bridge was built for $35 million and the San Francisco-Oakland Bay Bridge was built in less than three years for $75 million dollars, 1937–38. No EIRs!

Now, just a little comment on current infrastructure policy:

1. In 1950 the fuel tax in California, set by the legislature, was 4.5 cents per gallon of gasoline. At the aforementioned 1,000% inflation rate over the last 50 years, those 4.5 cents should be 45 cents per gallon. Fur-

ther, our present 18-cent per gallon rate set in the '80s has continuously gone down. Miles per gallon have doubled since the late '70s and inflation has increased about 300%. Thus the real fuel tax has gone down to an effective rate below five cents per gallon. Roads have also eroded.

2. Interestingly, the annual amount of revenue loss occasioned by the car-tax reduction equates with our present ongoing structural deficit—$4 billion cut for the last four years equals the $16 billion deficit. Adding to that irony, this in lieu property tax is federally deductible. California vehicle owners, corporations, commercial users, and all others who itemize have lost up to $4 billion of deductions over these four years and thus they/we pay the IRS up to $1 billion in increased federal income tax per year (at a 25% rate).

Perhaps that helps Congress earmark transportation money all over the nation. Give these facts some thought—Let's rebuild California. For some irrational ideological reason, a band of conservative Republicans, who believe in and foster investment capital, consistently oppose bond issues to invest in infrastructure and fuel taxes to build roadways.

12. Gerald Ford Remembered
Upon His Demise

Allow me some time to salute and write a tribute to President Ford—probably the most "real" person in any high public office that I have ever met. We last saw each other at a Bohemian Club encampment. He was so gracious, remembering me, recalling details about the Commodity Futures Trading Commission and his 1975 appointment of me as the first chairman.

I first met Congressman Ford on the "chicken and pea" circuit, participating with him when he was visiting California circa 1970. Humble and unpretentious, he was a totally sincere and friendly guy. I had traveled with Dick and Pat Nixon (1962) and with Nelson Rockefeller (1964). Nixon was smart but introspective. Rockefeller was a gregarious, huggable bear (we did not hug Nixon). But Congressman Jerry Ford was helpful, accommodating, going out of his way to offer help, political advice, and indicating personal concern.

I next saw President Ford in 1975–1976. My wife Diane and I danced at the White House; I briefed both the president and then Vice President Nelson Rockefeller on regulatory matters. Again, President Ford was unpretentious, no ceremony, just friendly conversation. It takes a lot but I was humbled!

I have often wondered but never asked—why did he not wait until after the November 1974 election to pardon President Nixon, instead of in late September. We know the pardon cleared the then polluted political air and "cleansed" America. That was a great historical grant of absolution, but the public's reaction led to November losses—i.e., about 50 Republican House seats, and in California Hugh Flournoy's close loss to Jerry Brown (by 90,000 votes) for the governorship was attributed to the pardon. The presidency was lost to Jimmy Carter because of the pardon but also because Ronald Reagan ran against sitting President Ford in the 1976 primary!

Again, the pardon epitomizes President Ford's undiluted dedication to the high art of governance, unaffected by a calculating ideology. Had

GERALD R. FORD

August 24, 1999

Dear Bill:

It was great hearing from you. Your letter brought back
fine memories of your excellent service as the First
Chairman of the Commodity Futures Trading
Commission. I was proud to appoint you and I was proud
of your leadership.

I am pleased you liked my Op-Ed piece in the New York
Times on Affirmative Action. It has been extremely well
received nationally. I hope the federal judiciary will follow
the suggested answer on the constitutional issues.

Betty and I are in Beaver Creek/Vail until October. Hope
to see you on our return to Rancho Mirage.

Best regards,

Gerald R. Ford

Mr. William T. Bagley
Nossaman, Guthner, Knox & Elliott, LLP
Thirty-Fourth Floor
50 California Street
San Francisco, California 94111-4799

15. (previous page) Former President Ford endorses affirmative action.

*16. (above) At a birthday celebration for former Gov. Pat Brown, (from left),
Bagley, Mike Peevey, Diane Bagley, and President Gerald Ford.*

EDMUND G. BROWN
450 NORTH ROXBURY DRIVE
BEVERLY HILLS, CALIFORNIA 90210

April 25, 1985

Mr. William Bagley
350 McAllister Street
Room 5056
San Francisco, California 94102

Dear Bill,

Just a word to tell you that you were absolutely magnificient at the dinner. I think you know that old Governors go to many affairs, but I have never been to a better one in my very long and troubled career.

You are a great human being. I wish you would run for Governor!

All of the best,

EGB/jsc

---

17. Former Gov. Pat Brown wrote to Bagley in 1985 after Bagley served as master of ceremonies at a birthday dinner for Brown. President Ford spoke at the event, which supported the Pat Brown Institute. Brown closed his letter with, "I wish you would run for Governor!"

my Sacramento apartment roommate during the '60s (Assemblyman, then Controller Flournoy) won the governorship in 1974, much of our life would have been different—no Rose Bird Court, maybe even a Bagley Court. Though Jerry Ford seemingly created Jerry Brown, we don't have to pardon him. We just thank this wonderful human being for devoting his life to us.

13. Earl Warren and Arnold Schwarzenegger

Arnold Schwarzenegger was destined to become the Earl Warren of the 21st century—a progressive, problem-solving, California-building Republican governor—but for legislative ideological gridlock.

Earl Warren, 1943–1953, proposed a statewide health coverage plan. He started the postwar period of building infrastructure—schools, new university and college campuses, first known freeway, new bridges—that extended through to the Pat Brown administration, 1959–1967.

During and after WWII, California experienced a "continental tilt," from east to west. Population grew from 6 million in 1940 to 10 million in the early '50s. We passed New York as the biggest state during the '60s. Incidentally, Nevada had only 110,000 people in 1940!

Warren was truly bipartisan. During the cross-filing era, sitting Republican Governor Warren was effectively elected in June 1946 by beating all Democratic candidates in the Democratic primary, thereby becoming the candidate of both Democrats and Republicans in the 1946 November election.

The legislature was also bi- or almost nonpartisan as a result of cross filing. Districts were whole cities, whole counties; there were no caucus staffs beating partisan drums and no party aisles in the legislature until the arrival of the so-called "Prop. 13 babies" in 1978. Earl Warren even had a rainy-day fund of $75 million, a substantial part of a then $1 billion total budget.

Warren, as President Eisenhower's appointee (1953) became a progressive chief justice of the United States Supreme Court (*Brown v. Board of Education*, etc.), thus elevating Lt. Gov. Goodwin Knight to the governor's seat. Knight continued to build California, formulating the basis of Pat Brown's 1960 California Water Plan, a $1.75 billion proposition placed on the ballot by the legislature in 1959.

This record of bi- or nonpartisan programs, including efforts toward racial justice and equality, infuriated the right wing. The newly formed

John Birch Society sponsored "Impeach Earl Warren" billboards. Warren's health plan was called "socialism."

Republican U.S. Senator Bill Knowland, believing he could more easily ascend to the presidency from the governor's seat than from the U.S. Senate, forced Knight aside and became the "right to work" candidate for California governor, leaving an unfunded Knight to run for Knowland's old seat in the Senate.

That crassly forced switch to the right, plus the right-to-work initiative and another initiative to tax churches caused a massive upheaval. Pat Brown overwhelmingly became the second California Democratic Governor (after Culbert Olson, 1938–1942) in the 20th century. The Assembly switched from earlier 50–30 Republican to 45–35 Democrats, overnight, in 1958. The newly empowered Democrats promptly repealed cross filing.

Partisanship began to emerge. Jesse Unruh became really the first powerful Speaker in November 1961. Pat Brown continued to build California for our then close to 20 million people, but a faltering Brown and a Republican resurgence elected Ronald Reagan on a platform to cut, trim, and squeeze the budget and to repeal Fair Housing (the Rumford Act of 1963).

Reagan, however, doubled Brown's last budget from $4.6 billion to $10 billion in five years and (if I may) as assemblyman I saved Fair Housing by refusing to convene a repealing conference committee at the end of the 1967 session.

Ronald Reagan was not a conservative governor. To his credit, he turned his back on the right wing by signing the then most liberal "choice" bill in the United States, he endorsed the Equal Rights Amendment, and we (AB 1000, 1001) increased state income and sales taxes by two billion dollars to finance a $10 billion budget.

In this 21st century there may be another California right wing revolt, but for naught. Times and the political climate have changed drastically since 1958. Party ideologues in today's California are just counterproductive angry losers.

Part IV—The Way Things Got Done

(The following vignettes are a compendium of dictated material, some of which are repetitive of preceding items but are more fully explanatory of the subject events.)

1. Train Trips

Southern Pacific could not give you a free train ride. Governor Hiram Johnson had inserted the initiative and referendum into the state constitution, including a provision stating that officeholders automatically forfeited office if given a free ride on a common carrier, i.e., the powerful Southern Pacific Railroad, which had provided free transportation to legislators from southern California to Sacramento.

But legislative train trips were a nice institution: The train went to Chicago—it left Sacramento around 6 p.m. and SP would hook either the president's car or a private car on the back of the Chicago train, and go over the hill to Tahoe and Reno.

Wonderful steak dinners cooked by the porters for eight, nine, or ten legislators—always bipartisan. Then SP would drop the private car, we'd get off at 8 or 9 o'clock, gamble until two or three in the morning, then get back to the car at 4, sleep from 4 until 9, and get off the train back in Sacramento, returning from Chicago, and go directly to the legislature.

Wonderful trips! It simply wouldn't be done today, no way. Al Schultz, who represented the oil companies, would buy the tickets—10 tickets on a private car would cost maybe two or three thousand dollars; then another train trip for others a few weeks later. And the SP lobbyists were always on the train. We never thought we owed SP anything; it was just a normal event. Instead of having dinner in a hotel, we had dinner on a choo-choo train! All those things just happened; they were just a part of our collegial lives. Perfectly legal and much less expensive than nightly $3,600 per person fundraisers.

2. People Who Play Together Stay Together

There was a group of us who started a card game at the old El Mirador Hotel on N Street. It was in the penthouse of the El Mirador. After Artie Samish, the infamous liquor lobbyist, went to jail, some of these liquor-lobbying jobs opened up. Former Assemblyman Danny Creedan from San Mateo quit and took the beer people. Judge Garibaldi came up from Merced, and he took over the heavy liquor/distillery lobby.

Anyway, the former San Mateo assemblyman had a suite for his office; hell, he had the whole penthouse. It was almost like a dance hall with a big deck outside. You could have a barbecue. There were two or three bedrooms; it was the whole top floor of the El Mirador. It was left open on Monday nights—8, 9, 10 o'clock—we would start arriving. The bar was open, although we didn't drink much while playing cards.

This was a fairly heavy card game—hundreds of dollars were transferred. We had per diem checks, and every Monday you would get a per diem from the previous week. The first thing that would happen was that the per diem checks would go around the table with half a dozen different endorsements on them—the checks would go back and forth as they were won and lost.

Later on, the penthouse went to Kent Redwine, who represented the auto dealers and movie industry people. He just continued the same practice.

We did this for about 10 years—from 1964 until I left in 1974. We never felt beholden to anyone for leaving their penthouse open. It was just an office, basically, and we thought it was just normal—it cost next to nothing for the use of the room. The only costs incurred were once in a while when we would play all night and order breakfast in the morning. Wing Fat would come by at 11 p.m. with leftover Fat's restaurant food. He was the only nonmember allowed to play.

The players were myself, Bob Monagan, Jack Veneman (before he went to Washington), Hugh Flournoy, Bob Moretti, Willie Brown, Frank Murphy, Jack Fenton (who was the Majority Leader at one point), Waddie

Deddeh—the whole damn leadership of both parties were playing cards every Monday night because we had a convenient place to get together. The important message here is that people who play together stay together. We fought on the issues but we were friends; there were few cheap shots, no hit-pieces. Civility prevailed because the leaders of both parties gathered together for a weekly card game. The suite was the catalyst. Friendships trump cheap shots. All of this was ruined by Prop. 9—political reform abolished camaraderie—and by Prop. 13—which led to the rise of ideologues, partisan aisles, and party voting when the ideologues took over.

On occasions we would go straight to the Capitol from the hotel, shave in the Capitol garage, wash up a little bit, and then go up to Ways and Means meetings on Tuesdays without any sleep!

3. Still on the Subject of Card Games: We Got Smart

Bob Moretti became Speaker in 1971 and Willie Brown became chairman of Ways and Means. Willie worked like hell. He was one of the smartest chairmen. Ways and Means hears every bill of any consequence, any bill with any money in it. There are hundreds of bills that go to Ways and Means—Willie knew every bill, he knew everything that was going on.

Willie knew more about the bills than the authors did. Fascinating. But he didn't want to stay up all night playing cards and then run Ways and Means. So when he became chairman of Ways and Means in 1971—he changed Ways and Means to Wednesday; for the card games continued on Monday nights!

And to this day, Ways and Means still meets on Wednesday, and that's why. We didn't change the card game—we changed Ways and Means, now called "Appropriations."

In many political books about politics, there is an allusion to this quote: "Those who like laws and sausages should watch neither of them being made."

The quote is ascribed to Bismarck, a Prussian. And there's some truth to it—120 people with all these diverse forces and vectors converging and then merging in Sacramento, a microcosm of California. It's just like sausage. You mix it up and put skin around it (i.e., sign the bill), and it becomes law. This worked well during the Golden Years.

Like it or not, poker has always been a political cathartic, cleaning up ideological obstruction and facilitating formulation of policy and programs.

In Robert Novak's book, *The Prince of Darkness, 50 Years of Reporting*, (p. 262), the author writes: "In Springfield, Illinois, State Senator Barack Obama played 'Wednesday Night Poker' with his colleagues. Poker is omnipresent in politics."

4. About John Harmer and Howard Thelen

John Harmer had been elected to the state Senate from Pasadena, defeating then Assemblyman Howard Thelen. I don't remember the bill number, but remember the subject. It was a very good child education bill that someone had given him. It came over to our house, but we simply were not passing any Harmer bills. Period.

Thelen was a very decent rational conservative Republican. Harmer was a right-winger. Thelen had voted (with the unanimous House) commending liberal Phil Burton upon his election to Congress—a simple courtesy resolution. Thelen also voted for a modified version of the Rumford Fair Housing bill. In the first of hit-pieces used during these times, Harmer published a campaign cartoon showing a black family moving into a Pasadena home saying, "Howard Thelen and his friend Phil Burton say I can buy your home!" This was a new kind of politics by a new breed, the paid aggressive campaigning pro. "I's yo' new neighbor" was another quote from the Harmer political cartoon.

But we saved the education bill for the education sponsors. We amended the bill on the Assembly floor, changing the author's name to Senator Schrade—a Harmer "enemy"—and sent it back to the Senate for concurrence in this one Assembly amendment. The Senate concurred and the bill is law.

We did this for Thelen and the good government bill, but actually to put down the Harmers of the world. We were colleagues working together. Phil Burton, by now in Congress, prevailed upon Pat Brown to appoint conservative Thelen to the court in Los Angeles County. That would not happen today.

5. The 10 Commandments—Are They Divisible?

Postwar, we had what we called the continental tilt—six, ten, sixteen million people, a mass of people, an infusion of people into California. It really occurred to a large extent along—and I don't know if anyone besides demographers knows this—latitudinal lines.

It makes sense. If you were from Maine or Michigan, you ended up in Marin County or San Francisco—temperate climate and all that. And if you were from the South, you ended up in Bakersfield, Orange County, or Long Beach.

That's how some of the redneck/John Birch Society aspects of Orange County, Bakersfield, Riverside, and San Bernardino counties came about—these were southern whites, southern Baptists, if you will.

In the late '60s, coming from this context or background, a religious-sponsored Senate bill is introduced to print a "moral code" in the front-piece of every elementary school book. Passing the Senate on a split vote, the bill is referred to the Assembly Education Committee. A proposed Assembly amendment would require the inclusion of the 10 commandments. Outrageously unconstitutional, but soon it was on the Assembly floor ready for a vote, being presented by Assemblyman Bob Badham (D-Orange County). The bill might pass and Governor Ronald Reagan might just sign it. Assemblyman John Vasconcellos (D-San Jose) was speaking eloquently about church/state separation but no one was listening. The bill might pass.

It is thus that I rose to ask, "Is this question divisible?" It was a single bill and could not be divided—but we had the House's attention when I moved "to divide the question on these commandments, there are at least two of them upon which I cannot vote!" A nervous titter ran through the House. Members started to laugh. I believe it was John Burton who then moved to table the whole bill (send it back to committee). The acting Speaker quickly called for an "aye" vote and effectively killed the bill. We had killed the commandments and also saved significant ensuing legal bills had the bill been signed.

In those days, the media sat on each side of the Assembly chamber and we would communicate. Tracy Wood of UPI asked me on which commandments could I not vote. I said, "I know it's six but I'm not sure whether it's nine or ten." Some readers will understand this comment, regarding thy neighbor's assets.

6. The Rumford Fair Housing Act

We had one black legislator in 1963, Byron Rumford (D-Berkeley). He was a quiet black leader of the early '60's. Akin to Ralph M. Brown, he practiced his profession for a living—owned and operated a pharmacy in his hometown. The fact that he was also chairman of the Assembly Health Committee posed, in those days, no perceived or real conflict of interest.

During Speaker Jesse Unruh's second full term, the Fair Housing Act was to become most controversial and confrontational.

It is saddening to acknowledge that only four Assembly Republicans voted against housing discrimination in 1963—the remainder proclaiming the absolute sacrosanct status of ownership property rights, the right to discriminate.

I was one of the four. The others were Milton Marks (R-San Francisco), later a Democrat; Houston I. Flournoy (R-Claremont, Los Angeles), later state controller and almost governor; and dairyman Alan Pattee (R-Monterey), chairman of the Agriculture Committee, who passionately pointed to the portrait of Abe Lincoln hanging over the Speaker's podium during the debate.

Equally sad was the comment made to me by another member: "I don't understand your vote —you don't have any of 'them' in your district."

Then, in the 1964 Goldwater year, a voter initiative called for the repeal of the Rumford Act *and would have prohibited comparable future legislation.* It passed almost two-to-one, with only Modoc County bucking the statewide trend. The ballot measure was led and basically paid for by the California Real Estate Association.

The California Supreme Court declared the public "repeal" vote unconstitutional (*Mulkey v. Reitman,* 64 Cal 2d 529, 1966). The rationale, rather simple but somewhat contrived by the court, was and is that since the Rumford Act proclaimed a state policy against discrimination, to prohibit any such policy in the future was actually "state action" in favor of continuing racial discrimination, and thus was violative of the Equal Protection Clause.

In the 1966 campaign, Ronald Reagan "demanded" the simple repeal of the Rumford Act by legislators. In 1967, outright repeal was passed by the Senate and sent by Speaker Unruh to the Judiciary Committee. There we fashioned a compromise that the House sent to the Senate, which nonconcurred as expected. A conference committee was appointed late in the session; I was the chairman and I simply never convened the committee. Fair housing remains the law—anyone wish to repeal it today?

Interestingly, a comparable equal protection argument will be made in an attempt to kill Prop. 8, a prohibition on same-sex marriages, passed in November 2008.

It is relevant here to cite *People v. Hall*, 4 Cal. 399 (1854), an early California Supreme Court decision that reversed a murder conviction of a white defendant—ruling that a Chinese eye witness on the streets of Weaverville was really an "Indian" (and thus could not testify) reasoning that our Native Americans originally traversed the Behring Straits from China. The Court then applied this early California statute: "No Indian or Negro shall be allowed to testify as a witness in any action where a white person is a party." Murder defendant Hall was set free.

This Court opinion, written just 100 years before the U.S. Supreme Court's watershed decision in *Brown v. Board of Education*, continues with this rationale, at pages 404–05:

> We have carefully considered all the consequences resulting from a different rule of construction—the same rule which would admit them [Chinese] to testify, would admit them to all the equal rights of citizenship, and we might soon see them at the polls, in the jury box, upon the bench and in our legislative halls. . . . This is not speculation which exists . . . but is an actual and present danger . . . a race of people whom nature has marked as inferior, and who are incapable of progress or intellectual development beyond a certain point, as their history has shown, differing in language, opinions, color, and physical conformation.

One justice dissented but without comment.

Where the Court found evidence of the Chinese migration is not stated but today's DNA evidence indicates our "Indians" are really Siberian, having migrated first from Africa, then to the Mid-East to Kazakhstan near the Caspian Sea, and then north to Alaska!

Totally irrelevant, but while citing case law this next wonderful citation is passed on to all lawyers. It is for universal usage, to support any proposition for which one can find no case in point:

> That no direct authority upon it had been produced must be due alone to the fact that legal evolution had not progressed far enough to develop a needless precedent for a necessary conclusion.

Fields v. Michael, 91 C.A.2d 444 (1949). Just cite the case by name, at page 451, and let the reader then find this quote. You may anger the judge but it can be part of the fun practicing law.

Speaking of attorneys, here is an item of historical interest and present significance. In 1950, state bar membership was about 20,000. Graduating from UC Boalt Hall in 1952 (and passing the bar), my bar number is 23929. State population was about 10 million; today we have close to 38 million, and new attorney bar numbers start above 220,000. Likewise during the same period, alive and active membership has increased from roughly 15,000 to 150,000-plus: a 380% increase in population but a 1,000% increase in attorneys. There's a message there.

7. Reflections on Jesse Unruh and "The Lockup"

During the period of the Young Turks, Jesse Unruh rose to power, because he was competent and smart, yes, but also because of another old cliché of mine—politics and physics are similar in that vacuums attract.

The infamous liquor lobbyist, Artie Samish, had been dethroned, which means there was no longer anyone in the Third House to help elect the Speaker. Samish had been the money funnel, and he controlled the House. When Samish was sent to prison for tax fraud, there was a period of "good government" in Sacramento.

In the early '60s, Jesse Unruh became chairman of the Ways and Means Committee under then Speaker Ralph Brown. Ralph was not a political animal-type person. Jesse was. Jesse began to raise money for other candidates, and that was the first time in then recent history—I can't speak for the '20s, '30s, and '40s—that a member of the legislature became a money funnel, and, in turn, handed it out. No one else was doing it then, in the House.

In those days, you could raise a couple hundred grand and hand 10 grand to 20 people. Out of 80 seats there were only 10 or 15 that were really volatile or vulnerable in any given year. Thus Jesse put his people in office and Jesse became speaker.

As Speaker-in-waiting, Jesse had a special session of the Assembly called in November 1962 to elect him Speaker. He changed the rules. This is a fascinating story—Ralph M. Brown was from Modesto. Jesse, as chairman of Ways and Means, was instrumental in creating the Fifth District Court of Appeal located in Fresno, when no one said it was needed, in order to get Ralph Brown appointed to the bench in October 1962.

It was beautiful politics—but power went to Unruh's head, there is no question about it, and that caused us Young Turks—myself, Monagan, Veneman, Flournoy, Cologne—to come to the fore in response to Jesse's garrulousness, his arrogance, if you will.

Jesse became a friend of mine. I don't mean to insult him. He was competent and had many great attributes, but power went to his head.

When power goes to the head of a powerful leader and others find themselves voiceless, in a system where you are expected to have a voice, a rebellion may be in order. That is what happened in the Unruh-led Assembly, in a most historic and traumatic way, in late spring 1963. "We" counseled a revolt as Jesse Unruh locked us up from 6 p.m. until 11 the next morning. National Guard cots were placed on the Assembly floor. The membership that year was Democratic, 50 to 30.

We were four new members in our second terms. Jesse had just engineered the election of a minority leader of his choice, by "owning" a number of Republican members—which left us voiceless. But the budget was up for a vote, which needed 54, a two-thirds vote. Jesse fully expected "his" Republicans to vote aye without hesitation (the total budget was only $4 billion).

There was a separate education finance bill beginning to take shape in the Senate, and we suddenly took interest in its contents, wanting a voice in its process. Somehow we prevailed in a Republican caucus meeting, which requested the Democratic leaders to—literally—show us what was in the planned education money bill, before the budget vote.

Jesse was incensed. "His" Republicans had to vote for the budget, no conditions. When there were no Republican votes for the budget, a normal "Call of the House" was imposed calling all members. Those who had not voted were not allowed to leave. Jesse became angry, he removed some of "his" Republicans from their committee chairmanships, went to dinner, had an excess of alcohol, came back, asked the House Clerk to call the roll about 30 times over and over and then ordered those who did not vote locked in the chamber overnight. He had solidified "his" Republicans against him because of this arrogance and was almost deposed by his caucus.

Only two of us Republicans, Jack Veneman and I, were let out—to play blackjack and have a drink or two with Speaker Pro Tem Carlos Bee (D-Hayward) and friends in his office. Jack and I returned to the chamber but all the couches and cots were taken. A token group of Democrats remained in attendance. Pauline Davis, the only female member, gave us the key to the woman's (one woman) lounge. (We were prepared to sleep on the Speaker's podium.) Jack and I found comfort: two couches and bathroom facilities, including a pink birdcage. We slept four or five hours, answering morning roll call by sticking our heads out of Pauline's lounge located in the back of the chamber.

Around 11 a.m., sanity prevailed. Senator Joe Rattigan (D-Santa Rosa) came to the Assembly snack room (now the Speaker's office), showed us the education bill, and the budget then passed without controversy.

But Jesse suffered a major public reaction. For this, he got himself a front-page picture in *Life* magazine and a lot of bad publicity, which in turn changed him. After this, he lost 100 pounds, bought a whole new wardrobe, and became a new, svelte Jesse Unruh and became a new man. During his Speakership he led the House and the state by developing, authoring, and passing major civil rights and civil law reform legislation. He learned a lesson about the exercise of power that others should learn.

8. A Little Background to the Rise of Ronald Reagan and the Right Wing

The 1964 Nelson Rockefeller versus Barry Goldwater fight needs to be examined. Goldwater ultimately lost to President Johnson by 1.9 million votes in California, the biggest percentage loss ever.

In the primary, Jack Veneman, Hugh Flournoy, and I were carrying water in California for Nelson Rockefeller. Bob Monagan stayed out of the fight because he was going to be our Speaker. We wanted to keep him sort of insulated, so it was almost all of the Young Turks.

Anyway, we traveled up and down the state for Rockefeller for that whole primary period. We'd go into the legislative session, if convened, at 10 in the morning, check in, then leave at five after ten, go down to Executive Airport and get in chartered airplanes and fly all over the state for three months, March to June.

We were Rockefeller's people in California. He couldn't do it, so it was our job to get the press, visiting editors, and almost every editorial board in the state.

We lost that '64 primary election by about 40,000 votes. The margin was 80,000, so if 40,000 switched, you would have had Rockefeller as the nominee.

I blame that on Happy Rockefeller (Nelson had divorced, married a younger lady!), who had her baby on Saturday, three days before the June California primary.

Putting all that aside, the importance is that Ronald Reagan had his political genesis in the Goldwater campaign. By that time, the GOP was beginning to be controlled by the Goldwater operation.

Some of these people were absolutely nuts—and I mean that literally. Out of 80 Assembly seats, there were at least 30 or so that no Republican could win, even if the incumbent died or went to prison. You cannot win a seat in a district that is 80 or 90% Democratic. No one in their right mind

109

18. On Nelson Rockefeller's campaign plane—a group of moderate Republican legislators traveling with the candidate in the June 1964 primary. The top row is Hugh Flournoy and Jack Veneman. Bagley is second from the bottom. Rockefeller lost to Goldwater by just 30,000 votes; Goldwater then lost to President Johnson by 1.9 million in California in November.

would run for the seat, and therefore some people that did—and who were then the Republican nominees—literally weren't in their right minds.

The best specific example is the story, told previously in this book, of the battle over the Republican platform for California for 1964. It's a sign of how bad the right wing became. Some see a comparable ideological party infiltration, presently, by the so-called evangelical religious right.

30 Rockefeller Plaza
New York 20, N.Y.

October 8, 1964

Dear Bill:

As a token of my appreciation of all you
did in our joint effort in the primary and in
order to have at least a small part in your campaign
for re-election, I am enclosing a check to your
Campaign Committee which I hope will help insure the
victory that I so much want you to have.

With my very best wishes,

Sincerely,

Nelson A. Rockefeller

The Honorable William T. Bagley
592 Fairhill Drive
San Rafael, California

NELSON A. ROCKEFELLER

22 WEST 55ᵀᴴ STREET
NEW YORK, NEW YORK 10019

File—Bagley '66

October 31, 1966

Dear Diane and Bill:

    Thank you so much for your welcome note of the twenty-fourth, and for the generous contribution to my present campaign that you thoughtfully enclosed. I am most deeply appreciative.

    This is a rough, and in many ways confusing, campaign; the knowledge of your support and your continuing friendship gives me a great lift in these hectic final days.

    With much gratitude and best regards,

        Sincerely,

The Honorable and Mrs. William T. Bagley
316 Alpert Building
San Rafael, California

19. *In 1964, Bagley, a lead Nelson Rockefeller supporter, traveled California with the presidential candidate, who lost the primary to Barry Goldwater. Rockefeller sent Bagley a campaign contribution. In 1966 Bagley, in turn and for fun, contributed to Rockefeller, who was running for his third term as governor of New York.*

9. How Ronald Reagan Became Governor of California

Stu Spencer and Bill Roberts, who had run the Rockefeller 1964 primary campaign, suddenly became the Reagan campaign management team in 1966, which incensed those of us who had worked for Rockefeller.

Somebody down South got awfully smart in the early Reagan "Kitchen Cabinet," and hired them.

Spencer and Roberts tried to insulate Ronald Reagan from the Birchers and the bigots. These far right-wingers were the people who would cry out: "Get the U.S. out of the U.N., and the U.N. out of the U.S.!" They'd scream: "Impeach Earl Warren!" etc., etc.

Nonetheless, Ronald Reagan did not win. Pat Brown lost. Pat had been in for two terms, he was at the end of his trail, and he lost. Ronald Reagan came into office in 1967 with a near 900,000 vote margin and brought new Republican legislative seats to us.

There were many, including Unruh's crowd, who feared a Brown loss in Pat's bid for a third term, claiming that he, Pat, had promised not to run, thus allowing Unruh a shot.

10. How Pat Brown Smeared George Christopher and How This Came Back to Haunt Him and Change History Forever

Governor Pat Brown and his chief strategist Don Bradley thought that Ronald Reagan, Goldwater's 1964 spokesman, would be easy to beat, so they wanted to get rid of former San Francisco Mayor George Christopher as a potential candidate.

The 1966 primary polls were actually showing at the time that Christopher was ahead of Brown, whereas Reagan was losing to Brown in hypothetical match-ups.

So Bradley enlisted syndicated columnist Drew Pearson to do a smear job on George Christopher. George, a dairyman, was convicted of putting too much cream in the milk in 1938 in Marin County. Because there was price control, you could not lower the price but instead he put more cream in the milk, avoiding the depression price control law.

George had violated the Milk Act; there was a photo of George Christopher in Marin law enforcement files with a criminal number under his mug shot. It was only a misdemeanor, but his photo was taken at the courthouse jail.

Drew Pearson ran the story via Fred Bagshaw, who was a relative of Marin D.A. Al Bagshaw. Fred got the old file from his nephew Al and sent it to Drew Pearson through Don Bradley. Pearson then wrote a piece about this candidate who was a "criminal," in his Washington, D.C., column.

Some California papers wouldn't run it; they were rightfully outraged by the article.

So then Drew Pearson flew out and held a press conference in L.A. and San Francisco. He held up a blow-up photo of George Christopher's "criminal" mug shot with a number under the photo, showing it on television.

At that point, Christopher and Reagan were virtually tied in the Field Poll, in April of 1966. After this fiasco, Christopher trailed by more than 10 points because of this diabolical Democratic attempt to get rid of George Christopher. They were successful, and Reagan's rise to power was the result. Absolutely true, that changed history!

11. The First Few Sour Days of Reagan's Governorship

This was going to be an interesting transition, to say the least. Reagan viewed the legislature as the problem.

Remember, Reagan won by running against Sacramento, much like Jimmy Carter had won by running against Washington, until he fell flat on his face when he couldn't make it work.

Even though some of us were a little bright, if I may say so, and we knew what was going on in our world, we simply weren't trusted. We were the problem.

In this sense, the party is totally incidental. In the minds of Reagan's people, everybody in Sacramento was either an old hack or a dirty liberal.

Reagan was surrounded by young men and women who listened to the campaign speeches, who were the advance people and the campaign strategists, and they were totally convinced that, number one, we were the problem, and, number two, all they had to do was march around Capitol Park on their white horses and solve the problems.

The first two years of his administration were an abomination, an absolute abomination. Gordon Paul Smith, who was the first director of finance, was going to cut 10% across the board, which is the worst kind of government. He had his figures entirely screwed up; you can't cut 10% from 70% of the budget, these are already mandated expenditures.

At one point, his figures were so screwed up, I declared there was an official "Gipper Gap" in Sacramento. This was early Reagan. We were trying to be helpful, but we were excluded. It was just like back in the Unruh days—they were not going to listen to any of us.

I can specifically recall a meeting he summoned—a Republican joint caucus with the Senate and the Assembly down in the governor's anteroom. His people wanted to discuss a budget problem. Finance Director

Gordon Smith said: "It's going to be a little tough, but to quote Knute Rockne, 'When the going gets tough, the tough get going.'"

At this point, I damn near threw up. Involuntary muscular contractions of the stomach took over, and I said: "Governor, Knute Rockne doesn't have any votes upstairs."

Governor Reagan initially exhibited a total lack of comprehension of the system, a lack of comprehension of the separate branches of government, as if the legislature didn't exist. This was a time to work with the legislature, with us and the then Democratic majority.

Yes, there were some dolts and a few crooks upstairs, but, God bless it, you work with them and you make the system work by compromising. That's why, with Reagan's disregard of this common sense truth, his first two years were an abomination. In a sense, the same syndrome existed during the first two years of Arnold Schwarzenegger's postrecall term. He was captured by some prior Gov. Wilson staff folks who drove him to try to act unilaterally, adopting Wilson's leftover causes instead of working the system.

We did, however, pass Governor Reagan's first tax increase in 1967.

12. On Some of Ronald Reagan's Inner Circle

Caspar W. Weinberger, a very bright San Francisco attorney, had been an assemblyman (1952–1958) and as State Republican Chairman (1961–1962) had endorsed former Vice President Nixon for governor—against the Bill Knowland/Barry Goldwater forces led by Assemblyman Joe Shell in 1962. This made him "a liberal," and the original L.A.-based Reagan "Kitchen Cabinet"—Henry Salvatori, Holmes Tuttle, Cy Rubel, and Justin Dart (major donors)—would not allow newly elected Ronald Reagan to appoint the government-knowledgeable Weinberger as his first director of finance—too liberal.

That is how Gordon Paul Smith came in as the first director of finance. Two years later, when Cap came in as director of finance, you can begin to chart the slow metamorphosis of Governor Ronald Reagan.

Ed Meese looms large here. Ed had been a lobbyist. He had also been a deputy D.A. out of Alameda County, and ever since the Earl Warren days, Alameda County supplied a deputy D.A. to lobby for the D.A.'s and the sheriffs' associations.

Ed had that chore and he knew his way around the legislature. He was not a happy-go-lucky, backslapping lobbyist, but at least he knew his way around. With the first wave of people leaving—and then with some of them learning—and with the ascendancy of Ed Meese, the atmosphere changed.

Now, please understand, Ronald Reagan did not have an evil bone in his body. He was not conspiratorial. I have never heard him say, "I am going to get that person," unlike Nixon, who was out to get his enemies.

And when I say Nixon, I mean that whole last part of his administration—the Haldeman, Ehrlichman, Mitchell, Colson gang—were out to get people. Never did I see Ronald Reagan having this "get" mentality. It's probably because he was stable. He was not insecure.

Governor Reagan had that as a plus, and then we began to see some of these people around him—Meese being my prime example—come to the fore and start saying, "Hell, we've got to make this system work. We can't just sit around and fight our little ideological fights."

Ed Meese is not an ideologue. He is a thoughtful conservative. An ideologue doesn't think, some can't.

Thoughtful Phil Battaglia was a key advisor. George Steffes was a good soldier during this time, trying desperately to "go upstairs" as legislative secretary and "explain the idiots" to Governor Reagan downstairs. Of course, we were the idiots upstairs. That was the context of government in 1967.

Ultimately, after a period of two or three years, Verne Orr came in to follow Cap Weinberger's brief stint as director of finance—Cap went to Washington when Nixon appointed him chairman of the Federal Trade Commission and then OMB (Office of Management and Budget) and then Secretary of HEW and Secretary of Defense.

Verne had been director of Motor Vehicles, but prior to that he had been a car dealer and an officer of a savings and loan in Pasadena. So he came in from a business background.

Verne was one of those people who literally came upstairs. He would come up at 6:00 at night, and put his feet on my desk. I would pour him some lobbyist's booze; we'd have a half dozen guys in the office, Republicans and Democrats.

He'd look up at my picture of Ronald Reagan in an Afro (a cartoon that I hung on my wall), and shudder, but at least we'd get something done. We put a $2 billion tax bill together that way. It worked with the new (1969) director of finance. Legislators want to be included in the overall process. Verne Orr knew that. We started to govern.

20. At a news briefing, Bagley makes a point while Gov. Ronald Reagan and Assembly Speaker Robert T. Monagan listen.

13. Republican Speaker Bob Monagan Confronts Republican Governor Ronald Reagan—Plus, Passage of CEQA

In January 1969, Bob Monagan became Speaker of the Assembly. We had achieved a thin 41-vote Republican majority. At that point, Nixon was elected. Jack Veneman had left for Washington to be Undersecretary of HEW with Lt. Gov. Bob Finch. Ed Reinecke was appointed lieutenant governor, and within the first day of his appointment, took a cheap shot at Veneman. (Reinecke was later convicted of perjury and resigned.)

Monagan became Speaker. I took over Jack Veneman's committee, Revenue and Tax. I had been chairman of Judiciary under Jesse Unruh in the last two years of his Speakership when Jesse had a 42–38 house—we were finally given a voice on the natural, not because somebody sold out. That's the good effect of an evenly balanced legislature: 42–38 either way makes for good government, bipartisan chairmanships on the natural.

One day in early January 1969, Speaker Monagan went down and broached Governor Reagan in his den and said: "I'm the Speaker, you're the governor. We're going to get along. We might be runnin' for president!" That was just about the time when the governor's people began to understand that they really ought to get along. So that was another catalytic event. Transforming Reagan, Bob Monagan gets the credit; presidential plans started to dance in Reagan's (and his staff's) eyes.

The governor, it should be mentioned, as is typical of new administrations with a business bent, formed a whole bunch of task forces, dollar-a-year kind of persons who were going to come up and do all of these great things. I can't name one thing that they were instrumental in putting together. But this changed when the governor's office and the legislature started policy discussions—taxes, welfare, environment—in 1969, together.

A mention of Bob Monagan (R-Tracy) brings to mind the passage of the California Environmental Quality Act (CEQA) in 1970, the supposed counterpart of the new National Environmental Protection Act (NEPA). NEPA requires an environmental study be performed prior to construction of a federal project.

Speaker Monagan had but two professional staff, Ed Rollins now of D.C. and Al Lipsom from the Rand Institute. Lipsom proposed the CEQA legislation to Monagan who literally went down the hall to Jack Knox's office (D-Richmond), then chairman of what is now the Local Government Committee. Bob said to Jack—you develop and author the bill, I as Speaker will be your co-author.

A quote from Monagan's book, *A California Solution* (p. 104), is most illustrative. Speaker Monagan, progenitor and prime co-author of CEQA, writes: "Projects meant construction, as in NEPA, not proposed changes in operating schedules, a change in hunting seasons or a change in (zoning) boundaries." But the California Supreme Court in the Mammoth case ruled that all kinds of newly proposed governmental actions, just to be considered, are "projects" and thus all need environmental studies. The court created a monster in Mammoth, possibly calling for the killing of more trees to print reports than saved by the act itself.

14. Reagan's Tax Revision and the 1970s Surplus

Ronald Reagan's 1966 election speeches promised to cut, trim, and squeeze Pat Brown's $4.6 billion budget. To avoid a tax increase, Pat's June 1966 budget (passing, of course, with a few needed Republican votes) advanced the collection of the next ensuing July's sales tax counting 13 months of projected revenue to provide an "extra" one-half billion dollars for the prior year. Some of us objected; jokingly, we proposed advancing the collection of the state inheritance tax—"Pay Now and Go Later," we said.

Governor Ronald Reagan took office missing the already used July revenue but found he could not cut or trim or squeeze $500 million of expense. He thus proposed and signed his first tax increase bill adding the 8% income tax bracket to balance his first budget—1967.

Now, jumping ahead, we proposed in '69 and '70 the identical elements of AB 1000 and 1001 in both years—authored by myself as chairman of Revenue and Tax, which finally passed in '71.

We increased the sales tax, virtually doubled the corporate tax, and added the nine, ten, and eleven brackets (having already added the 8%). We narrowed the brackets, made California the most progressive in the nation (and, of course, remember Ronald Reagan was against progressive income tax in 1966.)

This, in turn, spawned Proposition 13, because in the late '70s we had a tremendous surplus after national inflation went from about three to 10, 11, 12, and 13% a year. California experienced a major over collection of income taxes, progressive income taxes.

Narrowing those brackets and adding the brackets meant that everybody ended up in the higher brackets. That caused the 1978 six billion-dollar surplus, which in turn, together with inflation of property values, further fueled the surplus. So . . . we made California the most progressive income tax state in the nation under Ronald Reagan and literally "caused" Prop. 13. It's all "my fault"—we should have indexed the brackets to track income inflation, and thus have prevented this huge bracket jump.

While on the subject, let's address some aspects of Prop. 13 that are not often mentioned. Prop. 13 desecrated "Home Rule" in California. You no longer hear the phrase when discussing local government. It also concentrated power in Sacramento—certainly not a conservative concept.

Ronald Reagan's budgets in the '70s hovered above 10 billion dollars—the 2007–2008 total budget is $140 billion. That is a 1,400% increase in 35 years. Though the state has basically doubled in population since Prop. 13 (1978) and inflation has had a significant impact, a huge part of the growth of state expenditures—taking over local education and health and welfare obligations—has been caused by Prop. 13.

15. How Income Tax Withholding Built the Governor's Mansion

During the 1966 gubernatorial campaign, Ronald Reagan said, "Taxes should hurt," and he certainly would oppose income tax withholding that had been federal for decades—it reduces tax cheating. Now, in 1971, even though we passed the massive two billion dollar tax bill (on a 10 billion dollar budget), the state continued to run out of cash, i.e., 1971 income taxes were collected in April 1972. By December 1971 the state was ready to issue script—"tax anticipation notes" to pay the state's bills.

Ronald Reagan had to call a special session— late November 1971, to impose withholding, and he called me to introduce the bill—ABIX, "X" standing for "extraordinary" session (I arrived in Sacramento with shotgun and hunting clothes on my way to duck and pheasant hunting).

Immediately, new Democratic Speaker Bob Moretti held up the bill to pressure the governor (My AB2X would have printed Moretti's picture on the script). But we all knew instant passage was needed to protect the credit standing of the state. Director of Finance Verne Orr begged for instant passage in order to implement the bill with reporting employers by January 1, 1972. But what do you do with the "windfall"? The state collects 1971 taxes in April of 1972 but also collects three months of withholding taxes in January, February, and March of 1972, about an extra half billion dollars at that time.

The governor wanted to give taxpayers a half billion-dollar credit. The Democrats wanted to spend it. Ah, fodder for my compromise—spend $250 million on capital items only—school safety, and a "Bagley Conservation Fund" of $80 million. Verne Orr and I worked this out with Moretti in my office at 6 p.m. over some Lobbyist Garabaldi-supplied drinks— sergeants-at-arms brought ice. I had ABIX redrafted. On the way out of the office door, away from others, Verne asked me for "five million dollars miscellaneous construction." Okay, but for what I asked—for "a new governor's mansion," he responded. The mansion was constructed with withholding windfall but by then Governor Jerry Brown wanted to stay on his mattress on the floor of his apartment and drive his blue Plymouth automobile. No mansion for him; it was sold years later.

Note the above: how Governor Reagan and his replacement staff had learned the art of governance—to work together respectfully and get things done without ideological gridlock. One would think that rational folks first elected to high office would know this. But not ideologues and many times not those without governance experience. The latter risk getting captured by the former—i.e., Ronald Reagan and Arnold Schwarzenegger—in their first two years of governing.

There they were, arm in arm with Ronald Reagan in later years, meeting with Moretti, meeting with Leo McCarthy, meeting with the Democratic counterparts on the Senate side in our 1969–1970 tax meetings and in 1971–1972 on welfare.

On each issue, we met for a period of six weeks, one week solid with Reagan. Then we would meet with staff at night trying to get the bill into print for the next day or the next week. This went on for six weeks. Now, that's good governmental process.

This evolution of Reagan came about because he was finally beginning to realize that some of us were people worth dealing with, and, at the same time, realizing that he had to deal—just work things out together. How are you going to pass a bill? How are you going to balance the budget? How are you going to run for president if you can't get bills passed out of the legislature?

Reagan may never have admitted this evolution, but the fact is he was running for president in '68, then again in '76, and he wanted a record. It's that simple.

In negotiations, Gov. Reagan was pleasant, told funny stories and jokes, but was also tough. On occasion he would throw his horn-rimmed reading glasses and express disgust. "Stop reading *The Bee*," he yelled at me. "Only if you cancel *Human Events*," I replied.

But the process worked. Paraphrasing General Electric—Reagan's old employer—I pointed out that, in government, the process is our most important product. It is the process that produces results—good process equals good product!

16. The $2 Billion Reagan Tax Package—How the Bill Is Packaged and Jarvis Ruins Home Rule

Today it is hard to envision, in terms of a six-year term limit and the necessity for a two-thirds aye vote, how a near $2 billion new tax bill, 20% on top of a $10 billion budget, could pass—but that's what we did with my AB1000, 1001 in 1970–1971. It takes a combination of knowledge, trust, and guts internally among some and then between the many players. After many daily and nightly sessions over a period of two to three months meeting together, a dozen bipartisan legislators and Governor Reagan with a couple of advisors produced a conceptual tax package based on many compromises regarding "the incidence of taxation"—i.e., who gets hit where and who gets what back (inventory and property tax relief). These negotiating legislators must then mollify their peers so as not to upset other egos to obtain passage.

Today members don't know each other well enough to develop real bipartisan trust, and most members do not have the basis for being able to know who to trust and thus work with major interest groups—but that is the key to passing major general purpose nonlobby sponsored bills.

In 1970–1971, major interest groups played a major roll in rounding up votes—Republican votes were lobbied by the California Retailers Association, which wanted an offset—eliminate the local inventory tax—and Democratic votes were massaged by school groups and the UTLA union, both of which wanted school money. UTLA literally produced Senator Dave Roberts, the 27th vote. He had opposed a one-cent increase in the state sales tax. Even the oil lobby gave up opposition to increased oil levies, thinking there might be worse treatment. The process of bipartisan trust is foreign to members with only two or four years of experience and exposure.

So interest groups come in sideways and produce a vote here and there that helped to keep the package together and helped you tie the ribbon around the package.

As for how local government and county representatives fit into all this—the cities and counties really have a problem. They have no clout.

They have a great line— "home rule." But Howard Jarvis destroyed home rule in California by Prop. 13 in 1978.

The conservatives who supported Prop. 13 concentrated the power in Sacramento. It's that simple, and they destroyed the local option, local governance, and hence local ability to raise money and make decisions locally. The state picked up the local budget tab but also the budget power and authority. State budgets increased exponentially after Prop. 13 curbed local authority to tax.

17. Tax Reform as a Continual Process

What happens in these big bills is you have some ad hoc group of "legislative leaders." You don't go through the committee process as such; you negotiate an omnibus bill. By that time, with the Speaker in control of the committee—the bill just passes out.

We always had a couple of members who say: "Are we going to swallow this whole? We haven't had enough hearings. Who put this together?" So there is always the jealousy aspect.

But if you are going to get a package—the same thing is true, without equivocation, of the welfare package. Any major legislative package has to come through the side door having been packaged in another room. A consensus is needed.

You put your constituency together. You have retailers and you have your school people and you have your city and county people—you have everybody together. That was the key to our (my) $2 billion tax package—AB1000.

Earlier, Gov. Reagan came out with a tax package in '67. Gordon Paul Smith thought it up. Out of the whole gamut of interest groups—the cities, counties, schools, retailers, labor, manufacturers, all of your business groups of one sort or another—if there were 30 or 40 such groups, there was only one small group that came out for the package. Total amateur effort.

That was Reagan, circa 1967. No homework. No involvement of anyone either in the legislature or in the outside real world—coming up with a dumb package that everyone is opposed to except the Merchants and Manufacturers Associations that nobody has ever heard of. (Note: That is not the California Manufacturers Association.)

In major legislation, you have to work with groups. It's not obviating the system—there is still the committee system. It's not private, secret meetings, because you're not meeting as a committee. You're meeting as this ad hoc group that has collectively a whole bunch of antennae feeling their way through . . . and you put the package together. New term-limited members just can not do that.

You could almost call it a task force approach, but it is an entirely different sense of the term—not a bunch of amateurs, but instead, elected members, staff, and administration inside the system.

18. Welfare Reform Negotiations, 1971, and How Ronald Reagan Participated in Felonies

It's 1971–1974. L.A. Democrat Bobby Moretti is Speaker, and I am now chairman of the Assembly Social Welfare Committee.

When Moretti became Speaker, he had been working with some of us on all of the "Reagan" tax measures. It was natural, this bipartisanship. Bob called me into his office, and said: "Bill, I'm going to give six or seven Republican chairmanships. You can have your choice. Take whatever one you want of those that are left over."

I said: "I want welfare." He said: "You're out of your mind! It's a dog committee."

But I took it. John Burton was on the committee. Phil Burton, of course, had been chairman way back in '62. I was outnumbered—a minority chairmanship with Bill Greene and John Burton and three or four other liberal Democrats. The committee itself was of no use at all.

But I wanted the chairmanship because welfare was going to be the next big issue in the state, and if I had this catalytic role in taxes, why not in welfare?

So the exact same thing happened. We had meetings for six weeks in the governor's office. We put the plan together, and with Governor Reagan participating during the day and the staff during the night, we got it done.

I can remember buying 30 dinners for the staff; they didn't have any government money to buy dinners. We'd bring in sandwiches and beer, then work until midnight putting the welfare package together.

Now, Reagan never stayed until midnight, but he came in a couple of times at night during the tax package, the first time that we floated it in the late '60s. It passed the Assembly with Moretti's total cooperation, and we got up to 26 votes in the Senate where we needed 27.

Senator Tom Carrell had had a heart attack. Reagan came in all evening from after dinner at 7 until midnight, talking to Tom's doctor as to whether to fly him up in an ambulance plane, then decided not to.

Ronald Reagan was such a decent person. He told Senator Carrell's wife to "keep him at home, we don't want to risk his life for $2 billion." We passed the bill—converted into a Senate bill (SB90) a year later.

We committed some felonies, too.

I can specifically remember one sleazy senator saying he wanted his law partner appointed to the bench. I reported that as a fact, and the word came back, from Ed Meese, that, "We'll consider him." The senator also wanted $10,000 for his campaign (he had little opposition). I found a lobbyist whose group favored the tax package and I reported the request.

So I reported back to the senator, "You're going to get favorable consideration," and he cast the 26th vote for the tax bill, 27 needed. I honestly don't know to this day whether his law partner was appointed to the bench or whether he got his $10,000, but that's a felony. If you give someone 10 cents for a vote, that's a felony. If you give anything, it's a felony.

I said earlier we had a few crooks among the 120 members—the above is one of my best examples. Another example involved Sen. Randy Collier, chairman of Senate Finance Committee. A friend owned a small grocery store and had a problem with his liquor license, so I had passed a simple bill out of the Assembly—but Collier would not set it for Senate hearing. After weeks of waiting, I explained to Collier that there were no liquor interests involved, i.e., no "juice," only a clarification for a friend. I then gave Collier $500 in cash "for his trouble." The bill passed with ease, I had helped a friend but never told him this tale. I figured it was a campaign donation and reimbursed myself from my campaign account.

There are felonies committed every day in Sacramento— "If you help me over here, I'll give you a vote." That's consideration. It's a felony if there is a direct *quid pro quo* that benefits the parties. So we committed a few felonies in the course of human events, not involving cash payments.

They are not thought of as such, but technically somebody is asking to get some consideration for a vote. Consideration for a vote is a felony. Prove it.

So . . . Ronald Reagan was a peripheral participant in the prospect of committing a few felonies during the course of that era, as was, I'm sure—and will continue to be—every other governor. Facetious, but occasionally technically true.

19. One Whacky but Relevant Election of 1966

Hugh Flournoy (R-Claremont) was my Sacramento apartment room-mate during our sessions 1961–1966, elected with me, Gordon Cologne (R-Indio), and Bob Monagan (R-Tracy) in 1960. He was a Ph.D. professor of government but in 1966 could no longer afford to stay in Sacramento. Two days before the February 1966 close of filing, about 10 of us had one of our regular bipartisan dinners in the Senator Hotel, this one hosted in Jeff Peyser's hotel suite—The Wine Institute's lobbyist and a San Francisco attorney. Assemblyman Gordon Duffy (R-Hanford) kiddingly called Flournoy "a quitter." While playing poker after dinner, we talked Hugh into running for controller and collected $500 from Democrats and Republicans at the dinner to pay the filing fee. The next morning Jack Veneman and I filed Flournoy for controller at the Sacramento County Clerk's office, using the $500. Hugh woke up much later, spoke to his wife from our Thursday "Moose Milk" weekly open house and agreed to run. He had to sign "the papers"—we had already gathered 60 signatures and arranged for a Friday close of filing press announcement.

Importantly, note how regular, normal, ongoing lobby-sponsored dinners contribute not money but the basis for communication and, ultimately, bipartisan governmental action.

Recall the 1.9 million 1964 Goldwater loss in California. We did not believe that 1966 was a year to run statewide (I had decided not to run for controller). But Pat Brown had been weakened, lost to Ronald Reagan by 986,000, Bob Finch beat Lt. Gov. Glenn Anderson by 1,300,000, and Hugh Flournoy beat sitting incumbent Controller Alan Cranston by 40,000—votes coming in late on Wednesday, not election day.

We spent $15,000 in the Flournoy primary on part-time staff (Ed Slevin) and plane tickets to visit newspapers. Newspaper editorials were most effective in those days, when folks read papers!

As an aftermath, Alan Cranston was now out of office and took a flyer in 1968 by filing against the apparently unbeatable moderate Republican Assistant Majority U.S. Senate Leader Tommy Kuchel (a former state controller). But Kuchel was up-ended by right winger Max Rafferty in the

1968 Republican primary—thus Cranston beat Rafferty and was our U.S. senator for 22 years—Alan often thanked me in public for filing Flournoy in 1966 while he (Flournoy) was still asleep!

Another relevant aftermath: Eight years later, in 1974, Controller Hugh Flournoy lost the governor's office to Secretary of State Jerry Brown by 180,000 votes. Two major factors contributed to the result: Jerry Brown's sponsorship of "reform," Prop. 9, and President Ford's early pardon of Richard Nixon one month prior to the November election. Why not wait until after the election, was Nixon suicidal?

There are some fascinating campaigns in California electoral history.

Speaking of collegiality generally and Hugh Flournoy specifically, Jerry Waldie (D-Contra Costa), former assemblyman, majority leader, congressman, and presidential appointee, had this to say when Hugh passed:

Hugh Flournoy was a lovely man. Some of the best times of my political career were those spent in the Assembly palling round with Hugh, Bagley, Monagan, and particularly Jack Veneman. They were of course part of the opposition but what a wonderful part! Would that politics now and forevermore be patterned after those days.

Those were the Golden Years, enjoying bipartisan friendship.

20. Why Run for State Controller?

Why run for state controller? Because Controller Thomas Kuchel became a U.S. senator (1952–1968), and because Alan Cranston (former chairman of the CDC) became controller in 1958 and then (1968) became a U.S. senator for 22 years, and because Assemblyman Gray Davis (1982) became controller and then governor (not to mention almost-Governor Hugh Flournoy). There were others who tried.

The 1974 state controller campaign was interesting. For years, the state controller administered the state inheritance tax system (long since repealed) by appointing inheritance tax appraisers, at least one per county, whose percentage fees were based on the value of estates appraised. Amazingly, the "appraisals" and thus the fees included cash, bank accounts, listed securities, and already appraised real estate. These appraisers then contributed significant money to the state controller!

As assemblyman, I started a crusade in 1963 to change this system and to install qualified and salaried civil servant appraisers, saving state dollars. Also, noting the ongoing Democratic feud between Controller Cranston and Speaker Unruh, the bill obtained muscle support from Unruh (calling in missing votes at midnight) received massive editorial support but was killed in 1965 by Cranston's friends in the Senate. New Controller Flournoy and I killed the old "spoils" system in the late 1960s; Flournoy did not get enough credit for this real reform.

21. The 1974 Election and How It Led to Gray Davis Becoming Governor

In the 1974 election, Jerry Brown beat Hugh Flournoy by 180,000 votes (really 90,000 if those voters had switched) for governor. Third on the ballot, March Fong-Eu (D-Alameda County) beat Brian Van Camp (R-Sacramento) by 1.4 million for secretary of state. Ballot position is crucial. Next on the ballot for controller, Ken Cory (D-Orange County) beat me by 300,000. I did not escape the 1.4 million-vote deluge of Democratic support just above on the ballot. The major margin difference occurred because of newspaper editorial endorsements—about 100 for me, two for Cory. This included all major dailies, except one, the entire black press, the Latino press, the gay press—all for a Republican—plus the only time in history that Democratic clubs such as Alice B. Toklas (gay and lesbian club) and La Raza (Latino) endorsed a Republican! The Toklas charter was suspended by the state Democratic Council.

I then ran out of money, spending only $38,000 (my own funds) on statewide radio. Cory had spent $500,000 on television. But as a Rockefeller moderate Republican, I was the very last Republican to beat a Democratic statewide candidate in San Francisco.

Cory and former Speaker Jesse Unruh as the new state treasurer were sworn in together in January 1974. Cory jokingly said: "Jesse, we got all the (state) money."

As an aftermath, all of the above ultimately brought Assemblyman Gray Davis (D-Los Angeles) to the governor's office and then, literally, caused the recall ascendancy of Arnold Schwarzenegger to the governorship. On the last day to file for re-election as controller, Cory (who was experiencing some difficulty because of a Colorado oil scam PERS investment) called Gray Davis, said he was not going to file, and basically turned over the office to Davis to run for an open seat. Controller Davis later became Governor Davis.

None of that would have occurred had I been politically smart enough to spend time not "campaigning" among massive millions of people who are not worried about who is their controller, but collecting campaign dollars. There's another message there!

One final point about California campaigns: Before Prop. 9, contributors were not required to report their donations, and thus candidates could safely mis-report their contributions. The real plus of Proposition 9 was and is that all individual contributors must now report dollars contributed. That's the major benefit of political reform.

REAGAN
'.OR

State of California
GOVERNOR'S OFFICE
SACRAMENTO 95814

August 21, 1973

The Honorable William T. Bagley
Member of the Assembly
State Capitol, Room 2188
Sacramento, California 95814

Dear Bill:

This letter is to say thank you again for all the help
you've given me over the last seven years.

I am particularly grateful for your wise counsel and
vital assistance during the tax reform and welfare reform
battles of this period, culminating in major tax and
welfare reforms for the people. I am certain that the
monumental education finance and property tax relief
measure would never have come to fruition had it not
been for your untiring efforts. You managed almost
single-handedly to effect the necessary compromise
without sacrificing substance.

Again this year you have selflessly worked with me and
the legislature to defer the 1¢ sales tax imposition
which none of us wanted, and which you, with your inex-
haustible talent for finding workable solutions, have
managed to undo.

I sincerely hope that somewhere along the way you will
receive the thanks and gratitude which you so richly
deserve. I wish you all the best in the future, and
hope that you will remain in public life for a long time.

Sincerely,

Ron

RONALD REAGAN
Governor

21. A letter from Gov. Ronald Reagan to Bagley, thanking him for "all the help you've given me."

22. How Ronald Reagan Consolidated Turmoil and Becalmed the Body Politic

As governor, Reagan came to a controller campaign fundraiser held for me in 1974 at the Hyatt Union Square in San Francisco. Again, I was the amateur.

We didn't pull in a thousand people—we had 150. But Reagan showed up; he probably did more for Hugh Flournoy in terms of public appearances, but he certainly was not on the phone raising money for us.

Reagan was concerned about building a base for his presidential campaigns—I never had a conversation with him along those lines, but of course he was.

There wasn't an iota of scandal in businesses getting goodies or people getting goodies or someone getting a road paved to their lake or getting a special deal here or there, like highway contractors kicking back (which happens in other states around the nation). He ran a very clean administration.

You had absolutely none of that with Reagan, in part because he did have business-type people around him. I'm not advocating an aristocracy-type of government, but his people came out of an economic circumstance where they didn't have to, and had never really been exposed to cheap stealing, and because—to give Governor Reagan credit—he did pick some very decent people, other than those ideologues I spoke of earlier.

We went through the frenetic sixties with all of the civil rights activity, the Jack and Bobby Kennedy traumas, and Johnson's major legislative agenda. It might be said we needed a sort of plateau period where you didn't make major social progress.

We didn't repeal too much, but we consolidated and sort of kept the voters from getting overly agitated.

If this were needed at that point in history, Reagan certainly provided that kind of an administration, and that is definitely needed at times. You can't just keep hammering at the public to do new things all the time—you need a consolidation and you need a plateauing, a sort of becalming of the body politic.

There is a lesson in that somewhere.

22. Bagley with Bank of America lobbyist Hal Broaders, always good for a simple $200 contribution every two years. In 1974, "political reform" (Prop. 9) prohibited lobbyists from delivering contributions to candidates, which then led to the deluge of Capitol fundraisers seeking massive money from the same sources.

23. Campaign Contributions Prior to the Passage of Proposition 9—1974

In a classic application of one of the Peter Principles, the supply of campaign contributions then dictated the demand.

And the supply was dictated by known lobbyist budgets, which collectively would add up to $20-$30,000 in a given election for an "ordinary" Assembly incumbent.

Thus, the same amount was the average expenditure, governed by the available supply. Every member knew every contributing lobbyist's budget. That was the known limit; thus, there were no Capitol fundraisers like we have today.

Of course, there were exceptions. Senators received more than assemblymen; likewise committee chairs and other leaders. Nonincumbents did some early district fundraising, and the Speaker's funds were used in the right places for new member primary winners—hence, the continuation of the Speaker's power.

In the days of half-year sessions, the norm for the "ordinary incumbent" involved biennial visits from certain lobbyists, for example:

1. Hal Broaders, a former justice court judge, would "ride circuit" for the Bank of America. Every other year (for the Assembly), he would arrange a visit, maybe have a drink or dinner, and then hand over an envelope containing $200 in cash.

In 1964, Hal visited Senator Joe Rattigan (D-Sonoma) and me (R-Marin-Sonoma) at the same time. He met us during a League of Women Voters election debate at a Santa Rosa high school.

During a break in the proceedings, Broaders visited Joe and me in the high school auditorium boys' room, and there contributed to each with an envelope of cash. He was a great storyteller and a great friend, and the contribution was totally incidental.

2. Monroe Butler, lobbyist for Superior Oil, was more sophisticated and certainly more assertive. A perfectly dressed, white-haired gentleman (who did not drink and told no stories), he would summon members to his hotel room on a one-half hour schedule.

In the Bay Area, members would trek on a given day to the Mark Hopkins Hotel at the appointed time, ring his room, and then be greeted with polite conversation . . . and $500 in cash. I seriously doubt that anyone reported these cash contributions. It was demeaning but I joined the trek, every two years.

3. There were other cash contributions, but there were many other mechanisms. Cashiers' checks were popular, sometimes postal money orders, and then the smaller checks ($25 each) made out by a number of corporate executives. It was thus that one received PG&E's budgeted amount of $250 at $25 per management employee, reported individually. Again, no $3,600 per night fundraisers, just the biennial budgeted amount.

24. More on How Cash Cows Spilled Their Milk Prior to PAC Days in Sacramento

Again, since everyone knew the contribution budget of every lobbyist, and knew that nothing more would be forthcoming, there was no occasion for and there simply were no fundraising events in the Capitol.

If you were to have such a function, you would receive the same budgeted amount from the same lobbyists! There were no "independent" political action committees (PACs).

Lobbyist registration and campaign contribution reporting were in their infancy prior to the passage of Proposition 9. There was no reporting by the contributor; the candidate reported selectively. Cashiers' checks, if reported, could be (and were) reported as from the bank cashier, as if he or she were the personal donor.

Cash might be used in many ways and was never reported.

(On a subsequent contributor visit by Broaders of the Bank of America, Hal met me at San Rafael Joe's for a late evening drink. There, we encountered the entire Democratic County Central Committee, which had just met in the old San Rafael Courthouse. Using the newly acquired $200 in cash, I bought a series of drinks for the whole Democratic Committee, announcing that Speaker Jesse Unruh had given me—a Republican—the money!)

In this part-time era, the vast majority of members were truly citizen legislators, running their farms, drugstores, insurance agencies, or law practices by surrogates; and they would simply telephone their business dealings during the session. Wives ran the store in many instances—there were no wives in the legislature, and very, very few lived in Sacramento.

But there were a few members who literally lived on the $500 per month stipend, plus all the lobby/campaign cash and other monies that they could stash. For example:

In 1957, then Marin-Sonoma Assemblyman Dick McCollister (R-Mill Valley) made a deal with then State Democratic Chairman Roger Kent of Kentfield. If Roger would see to it that Dick had no Democratic opposition in 1958, then Dick would not run in 1960, leaving the seat open for a potential Democratic takeover.

Roger kept his word in 1958, but the same campaign contributions came to Dick from the same budgeted sources. Dick did not have to spend that money, as there was no campaign. Dick kept his word and the money, and did not run again in 1960. No illegality had occurred (assuming income tax payments were made).

I won the 1960 election, spending $7,000 ($3,500 of my money) in the primary and a total of $18,000 in the general election covering then 300,000 constituents in all of Marin and Sonoma Counties, from Sausalito to Stewarts Point in Sonoma.

Proposition 9 and ensuing FPPC regulations corrected most of the sleazy activities by requiring, in essence, double-entry accounting—triple, really. The donor reports and the recipient are impelled to report the same amount, and expenditures are reported to the nickel.

Had Prop. 9 stopped there, requiring and enforcing full disclosure of all monies (and had it not replaced known lobbyist money and forced the formation of impersonal PACs whose personnel and budgets were unknown to members), then campaign expenditures (following the supply) would not have exploded in post-1974 years.

Prop. 9 eliminated the lobbyist as the ostensible source of funds. Until the California Supreme Court declared otherwise, a lobbyist could not even recommend contributions to a candidate or member.

It was thus that a plethora of PACs formed to provide the campaign fodder from 1975 forward. And it was thus that members, who no longer were assured of the lobbyist budgeted amount, called upon the PACs for much larger contributions to be given at—for the first time—fundraisers in Sacramento.

Hence, the price of reform, a reform caused by President Nixon and by Jerry Brown. Nixon and Watergate spawned decades of suspicion and distrust of public officeholders, and thus government in general and campaign money in particular. Jerry Brown spawned Prop. 9, he helped write and, through the initiative process, passed Prop. 9 and, at the same time, used this public hunger for so-called reform to become governor of California.

Another effect of Prop. 9, this one intended, was to curb what was described as the insidious relationships between legislators and lobbyists. After 1976, registered lobbyists could spend no more than $10 per month on a member or any legislative staffer.

This gem of a law did nothing to curb lobby influence. PACs flourished and certainly were identified as an interest group, and, when necessary, the nonlobbyist vice president of the business or union would call the legislator for a $50 dinner and for a key vote. So—still free dinners, but no longer bipartisan friendship events.

What this seeming $10 limit did was destroy the camaraderie and even civility that had existed for decades. And to further reduce opportunities for communication and understanding and importance for trust, the weekly ritual of multidollar fundraisers are all partisan. Thus all organized gatherings are limited to same party members. Sad and destructive.

(Attorney General Jerry Brown, commenting on present Capitol operations, said recently: "Bring back Moose Milk!" A senior *Los Angeles Times* reporter echoed: "We need to reopen Posey's and the El Mirador Hotel.")

25. School Desegregation Guidelines—Another Attempt to Show That Some GOP Members Believed in Social Progress

In 1971, of my own volition, I came up with another idea for solving some problems—guidelines for school desegregation that Ronald Reagan actually signed!

There had been administrative guidelines in the Department of Education, and the Reagan-appointed State Board of Education repealed those guidelines.

I took those guidelines, changed them a little bit, and rammed them out of the legislature to become law. Those administrative guidelines had several purposes.

One was just to give guidelines to school districts as to what they should be doing. Number two—and this is why Ronald Reagan signed it—if you have an administrative process that you go through, you must, by 300-year-old Common Law, exhaust your administrative remedies before you go to court for an injunction.

By going through administrative guidelines and the administrative process, you would stop people from suing to force a school district one way or the other—and from Governor Reagan's standpoint and from Ed Meese's standpoint, this was one way to forestall the courts from taking over. So they signed the bill.

L.A. Assemblyman Floyd Wakefield called it the Bagley Busing Bill, and by God, he got three hundred and some odd thousand signatures and referended the new statute as Proposition 21. The proposition was overwhelmingly approved by the voters, repealing the bill.

An initiative passes a new statute, the passage of a referendum repeals an existing statute. The referendum was overwhelmingly passed, two- or three-to-one, because the guidelines were portrayed as a "busing bill" contrived by opponents of busing.

It was supposed to be the exact opposite. It was supposed to be exactly an administrative process —some guidelines as to when you do what and how you do it. And it was a process—meaning administrative procedure, hearings, etc.—where you apply certain standards. And all of that would have stopped lawsuits at least for a while and stopped the stridency of antibusing.

But that was repealed. It was an attempt to solve the social issue and also to try to show the general public that some of us in the Republican Party cared about that kind of social progress.

That was another element during this period of the Young Turks. We were trying to be progressive Republicans, and, in the end, basically lost every battle. We would win some of these central committee fights, but the end result is that you do not see a grassroots uprising of "evangelical moderates" in today's political society.

Over this last period of 30 years, the battle to maintain a strong moderate force in the organized Republican Party has been lost. So sad—and look at the declining registration, many changing to "decline to state."

It is dramatic. In 1960, 4% of the California registered electorate was "declined to state." Today it is close to 20% and rising. Party registration is declining but party voting primaries are becoming more and more partisan. The ideologues are winning.

26. Republican Fortunes in the Assembly in the Tidal Wave of Jesse Unruh's Democratic Stronghold

Gov. Hiram Johnson created cross filing in 1913, allowing all candidates to run in the primaries of all the parties. Voters could not tell which party a candidate belonged to, since there was no party identification on the ballot. That changed in 1952, when party designations were added to the ballot, and then in 1959 cross filing was abolished. But there was no party force as such until the Unruh speakership days.

The premise to all of that is that all during those years there were chairmanships from both parties, based upon a kind of friendship coalition. It wasn't a voice of the other party; it was whoever your friends were in the other party—someone who was going to support you, "sell out" to you if you will, or better, one with whom you wanted to work.

Later there were four or five Republican chairmen during the Jesse Unruh speakership up until 1966, but they were sell-outs. They were people who had made their deals, and Jesse needed a half dozen or so to ensure control, not ideological but on the budget and internal organizational issues.

You needed three or four on the other side to stop, for example, any kind of coalescence where one-third plus one would stop some two-thirds vote measure from going through.

Jesse was an artist in that regard. He had at least a half dozen Republicans in his pocket, and we did not like that.

So that is the genesis of a new resurgence of Republican effort and all of us moderate Republicans coming up with ideas of our own, challenging the administration, leading up to, without our knowing it, the Ronald Reagan campaign.

Bob Monagan, by this time, became Minority Leader in 1966. In '63–'64, Charlie Conrad was Minority Leader, and I mean this next sentence literally:

Jesse Unruh elected the Minority Leader.

We ran against Charlie Conrad, but Jesse had locked in Republican votes. To make a long story short, they supported Charlie Conrad who was Jesse's candidate for Minority Leader.

Very few of the dealmakers were openly honest, a quality not universally ascribed to elective officeholders. A prime and earthy example of honesty among colleagues was Alan Pattee (R-Monterey). Alan, a Harvard grad and successful dairyman, was chairman of the Assembly Agriculture Committee, appointed by Speaker Unruh. Earlier, Alan had committed to support Bob Monagan for Minority Leader in the 1963 session. But in late '62 he openly came to us, saying to Jack Veneman and me—and I quote—"You guys know me and what I like. As chairman, I get to travel and to drink and to screw—are you gonna take that away from me?" We understood and relieved Alan of his commitment so he could keep his chairmanship. I tell this tale to dramatize open honesty in politics.

Another earthy story, again with Unruh involvement, could be told explaining how then Attorney General Stanley Mosk obtained Pat Brown's appointment to the California Supreme Court instead of to a vacant U.S. Senate seat—but—for Stanley, I don't want to tell that tale.

27. One of the Downsides to a Professionalized Legislature

The growth of staff is outrageous—the bill numbers change, but the issues do not.

California has 38 million people as opposed to the 20 million at some point in time 30 years ago, but the fact that the population has doubled makes little difference.

The issues are the same; the arguments are the same.

We got along just wonderfully, colleagues trusting each other, working with each other, without the obstacle of three, four, five, six, seven, eight, nine, ten staff people.

Today, if you aren't in a position as an ex-legislator to be a friend of the legislator, you go to the Capitol, and you'll be swamped with staff—you'll hardly ever see the legislator, and that's too bad.

It was a much better system when we met for six months a year and we had one or two staff people rather than five or six or seven, each. But, admittedly, before Speaker Unruh, there was a dearth of staff—one half-year secretary per member and no professional help except for committee chairmen (all men). Lacking any internal help, the Los Angeles Republican Associates paid Sandy Quinn and Ron Ziegler (later President Nixon's press secretary) $500 per month to assist Republican members in 1961–1962. But—we did vote ourselves, some even read the bills. With Unruh as Speaker, if the Democratic Caucus obtained three or four staff positions, the Republicans got one. That was progress, but, again, the system worked better without today's grossly excess staff.

28. Underscoring Again How Proposition Nine Has Created Precisely What It Was Designed to Eradicate—The Proliferation of Campaign Contributions and Expenditures

This is not just me talking—if you talk to Bob Monagan and others who were there 40 years ago, you get the same reaction.

Proposition 9 (the Political Reform Act of 1974), which was designed to bring about campaign reform, passed as an initiative in 1974 and actually brought about the explosion of campaign contributions and expenditures it was designed to forestall.

It insulated the lobbyists for a couple of years until the Supreme Court acted.

The lobbyists not only could not contribute, but they also could not even give advice as to whom to contribute; the latter is unconstitutional. Lobbyist is not an evil word. Sacramento is a microcosm of every force in society, all the way from the Humane Society to the oil industry and the Catholic Church.

When lobbyists were excluded from the contribution process, a plethora of PACs was created. Again, politics and physics are very similar—vacuums attract.

There was a vacuum, so the outside world had to fill the vacuum. And the growth of PACs and campaign costs is absolutely cause and effect from 1975 forward, after Prop. 9.

The PACs are impersonal—you don't know who they are. All you know is you've got a whole pot of money in each of the PACs for all the industries and all of the labor.

And what you do—because you're not dealing with your friendly lobbyist whose budget you know, but with this impersonal PAC—is think: Why not get $10,000 from them? They've got the money, after all, and you don't even know who they are.

So you go after the money by having fundraisers in Sacramento the night before the bank bill comes up. That never happened before—and it's all caused by Common Cause and Jerry Brown, who sponsored Prop. 9 in 1974. And I mean that literally.

29. Whither Goes the GOP? To Withering Away?

One debate after the 2008 national election concerns the status, direction, and "re-branding" of the Republican Party because of the rapidly decreasing voter identification with the GOP coincident with the rapidly increasing number of independent ("decline-to-state" in California terminology) voters who simply must be attracted in order to win any general elections.

History is the ultimate teacher. Note this history recited in my *San Francisco Chronicle* op-ed piece on May 13, 2009:

The rise of the likes of radio talk-show host Rush Limbaugh as the vicarious voice of the Republican Party, the recent demeaning of former Secretary of State Colin Powell—a national hero—by ex Vice President Dick Cheney, and the continuing loss of registration and identity require us to ask: Whither goes the GOP? To wither or not to wither, that is the question.

As always, history should be our guide when we wonder what happened to the moderate middle in what was a winning party just a few decades ago.

During the Kennedy and Nixon years, there was an Eastern Establishment epitomized by Republican Gov. Nelson Rockefeller and demonized by Republican Sen. Barry Goldwater.

That establishment was propelled by a cadre of moderate senators: Ed Brooke of Massachusetts, Clifford Case of New Jersey, John Heinz of Pennsylvania, Jake Javits of New York, Hugh Scott of Pennsylvania, Lowell Weicker of Connecticut, and others, all Atlantic states Republicans. Add Chuck Percy of Illinois, Hiram Fong of Hawaii, and our own Tommy Kuchel, who served from 1953 to 1969. With the recent departure of Arlen Specter, now D-Pa., none of those states has a GOP senator today.

Further, in all of New England, there is not a single sitting Republican member of the U.S. House of Representatives.

Add more history. Reacting to the Johnson civil rights era, the Nixon forces in the personage of Attorney General John Mitchell instituted the "Southern strategy." It worked. Dissident semi-segregationist Democrats became Republicans and shifted the GOP base to the South, leaving eastern and western Republican states bare.

Now let us relate this to California. That history did not teach California's Republican voters a lesson in survival. Note what follows:

• 1958: Sen. Bill Knowland running in an antilabor "right to work" platform ousted sitting Gov. Goodwin Knight, who then ran for Knowland's U.S. Senate seat in the primary. Both lost big in November. The state legislature then turned Democratic for only the second time in the 20th century.

• 1958–64: San Francisco successively had a Republican congressional representative, Bill Maillard, and Republican Assemblymen Caspar Weinberger, John Busterud, and Milton Marks, all long gone.

• 1964: Goldwater beats Rockefeller in the primary but then loses to Democrat Lyndon B. Johnson by 1.9 million votes in California. Right-wing delegates proposed a platform plank to "send Negroes back to Africa," forcing the state Republican Convention to adjourn without a platform, for fear of passage after sane members had left for dinner.

• 1968: Sitting U.S. Sen. Kuchel, earlier appointed by Gov. Earl Warren, is defeated by extremist Max Rafferty, leading to Sen. Alan Cranston's 22-year Democratic reign.

• 1992: U.S. Rep. Tom Campbell's narrow primary loss to right-winger Bruce Herschensohn brings Democrat Barbara Boxer to the Senate.

• 2002: Bill Simon beats moderate Los Angeles Mayor Dick Riordan and then loses badly to Gov. Gray Davis.

• 2009: The now very right-oriented Republican State Committee, risking huge deficits and dumping of California credit, opposes all compromise budget propositions on the ballot.

So sad, no lessons learned.

Until the present decade, the state legislature was run by moderates of both parties. On the Republican side, we would seek budget cuts, achieve a few million dollars in cuts, then vote for a new budget and claim victory. Moderate, problem-solving members prevailed.

The risk now is further contraction of what really was a Grand Old Party and thus a further self-defeating movement to the far right in the name of "purity."

The broader message for both parties is: Beware of ideologues bearing seeming gifts.

Perhaps a more pleasant point for Republican voters is to be reminded of the enormous, 49-state loss of the left-leaning Sen. George McGovern to President Nixon after the 1972 takeover of the Democratic Party by McGovern forces. That is a lesson for both parties.

Reprinted with the permission of the *San Francisco Chronicle*.

PART V—There is Life after the Legislature

1. A Tiny Slice of Life as Chairman of the Commodity Futures Trading Commission

One quick little story:

We had a large staff of about four or five hundred people spread around in Chicago, New York, Minneapolis, Kansas City, San Francisco, and Washington, D.C.—two to three hundred in Washington.

So Joe Mink, our property manager in Washington, was helping us move into our new building, which had a lot of balconies.

I said to Joe: "Give me the key. I want to open the balcony."

And he said: "Oh, I hate to give you the key. The last building I managed, one of the commissioners jumped out the window."

I said: "Why don't you give the other four commissioners the key instead of me, then?"

2. Throwing Red Tape into the Potomac . . . Literally

One thing I learned as the first chairman of the Commodity Futures Trading Commission (1975–1979) is that if you are a staff-level bureaucrat and you possess a "confidential" stamp, that's probably a sign of authority.

These people are accustomed to having a little stamp so they can stamp "confidential." We didn't have any provision for it, and there wasn't any delegated authority to others to stamp things "confidential."

So people went out and bought their own blessed stamps so that they could write memos to me as chairman, and stamp them.

Out of the blue, I started getting these four, five, ten-page memos stamped "confidential." This was absurd. In effect, it was counterproductive, too, because if you stamp something "confidential," then people want to look at it.

I told our property services manager, Joe Mink: "Joe, go around this building and get every one of these 'confidential' stamps, and put them in a plain brown paper bag, and deliver them to me. I shall deep-six them in the Potomac River."

Well, that became something of a joke around the office. Joe brought me these little "confidential" stamps, about 10 of them, in a brown paper bag. And someone said: "Are you going to deep-six them in the Potomac?"

And I said: "Sure, why not?" A photo was taken by UPI of myself on the Memorial Bridge throwing the stamps into the river.

The interesting thing is that the story never ran in the *Washington Post* or in the *Washington Star*. The farther away you got from Washington— we had a clipping service, and I have clippings of the deep-sixing that are two inches high—the bigger the story.

City editors loved the fact that somebody was trying to "de-confidentialize" government in Washington.

3. How Jimmy Carter Tried to Shoo Me Out of the CFTC

My term as chairman of the Commodity Futures Trading Commission was five years. I didn't go back to D.C. to be a career person, I went back because—"If you play Peoria, you want to play Broadway."

In the meantime, 1976 came by—Ronald Reagan ran against then sitting President Jerry Ford (who had appointed me to the CFTC). Reagan caused Ford to lose; had Reagan not run against Ford in the primary, there would have been stronger support for President Ford in November.

But it didn't work out that way. Reagan played the spoiler; Ford lost.

At any rate, Jimmy Carter came into office. I still had a term of about three more years, and every few months a guy from the Carter White House would call me. His name was DeJong Franklin, a major White House Georgian, and he would ask in that charming southern accent: "Bill, how ya doin' over there?"

I'd say: "I'm doin' fine."

He'd say: "How's yer plans comin' long to leave?"

I had gone to visit him when the new administration took office—it's the custom as chairman of a commission to do so.

During our visit, I had said to him: "Yes, I'm not going to stay here. I'm going to leave."

So every six months or so, he'd call up and inquire: "So, how's yer plans comin' long to leave?"

Well, we had a four-year sunset on the act whereby Congress had to reauthorize the CFTC. Basically, I stayed three years and nine or ten months—stayed until we got reauthorized by Congress, and then I left in 1979.

And that was the end of that little stint.

The White House has a mentality—it doesn't matter whose White House it is, Nixon's, Carter's, or Reagan's. Maybe it can be "kinder and gentler," but they've got to play hardball. They've got to ferret out everyone who isn't one of theirs—in the Nixon White House paranoia prevailed.

That's why I had this cryptic little dialogue going on with Franklin—because we were the only commission around at the time Carter came in with five sitting Republican appointees. It was especially visible because the chairman was a Ford appointee, even though we were accused of being Nixon Republicans.

Anyway, we tried to accommodate. I got a call from Tip O'Neill, the Democratic House Speaker at the time, and he said he wanted his very good friend, Massachusetts Congressman Edward P. Boland, to get his wish—to have Boland's godson be general counsel of CFTC.

So that's how Jack Gaine, an active Democrat, served and served well as general counsel of the CFTC. I always tried to be ecumenical.

NOV 13 1984

THE WHITE HOUSE

WASHINGTON

October 18, 1984

I am delighted to send my warm greetings and congratulations to all those celebrating the tenth anniversary of the Commodity Futures Trading Commission.

Because of your devoted efforts during the past decade, CFTC has established itself as an efficient and effective regulator of the nation's commodity futures exchanges. As I stated a year ago at the swearing-in ceremony for Susan Phillips, the first woman ever appointed to chair a Federal financial regulatory agency, "This Commission is one of my favorites because it proves that government can do a good job without soaking up taxpayers' money or over-regulating the marketplace." Today, I extend that praise to all of you and applaud the diligence and creativity with which you have fulfilled your responsibilities.

Nancy joins me in sending you our best wishes for a memorable celebration and for continued success in the years ahead.

Ronald Reagan

23. *In 1984, President Reagan sent a message to the tenth anniversary celebration of the Commodity Futures Trading Commission, of which Bagley was the first chairman.*

4. How I Got Appointed to CFTC in the First Place

I'll start with that old saw of mine—"If you've played Peoria, you want to play Broadway."

Jerry Ford was president at the time. Donald Rumsfeld was Ford's chief of staff. Don was and is a friend of mine.

Through another mutual friend, a lady lawyer in New York who was one of then Vice President Nelson Rockefeller's main advisors, Rita Hauser, Don learned that I would like to come to Washington.

Parenthetically, I had talked to former California Governor Pat Brown about going into his law office. Pat had said to me: "We need you. My son Jerry's governor. I can't go to Sacramento anymore."

So, I was sitting with Pat in his law office in Beverly Hills on January 15, 1975, and got a call from the White House saying, in effect, "Please come back to D.C."

I went back to the White House and to the old Executive Office Building for an interview, and I was approached with being chairman of CFTC. And I remember thinking: "What the hell is that?"

It was explained to me that this was comparable to the SEC (Securities and Exchange Commission) for the commodity world. Actually, Joe Kennedy and William O. Douglas had been two of the first commissioners of the SEC.

I said: "Well, I don't climb mountains and I don't have a Scotch franchise, but I do have a young bride, so sure, I'll do it."

(Political insiders will not have to be reminded that William O. Douglas was a mountain-climbing husband of a lady many years his junior, and Joe Kennedy made his millions selling Scotch.)

5. The Commodity Futures Trading Commission

A diversion worthy of discussion here is how an entire industry expanded by volume of trading over 10,000% because of, not in spite of, "regulation" in Washington, D.C. The Commodity Futures Trading Commission is the counter-point of the SEC for exchange futures trading. For almost 100 years prior to the new 1974 futures legislation, commodity markets in Chicago traded "ag" futures—from soybeans to sowbellies—and were monitored by a bureau of the Department of Agriculture, which incidentally was a paying tenant located in the basement of the Chicago Board of Trade—which it watched. Congress created the new commission, led by industry lobbying, to give it omnibus power and to expand futures trading to include as a commodity "any item of goods or services traded on an exchange"—any item. Thus, new commission rules governing "contract markets" included futures trading in foreign currency, mortgage rates, S and P futures, other derivatives—a massive new industry created by Congress and a new regulatory commission that had the guts to approve the expansion.

But governance in Washington, D.C., in the executive arena, is a phenomenon unto itself. Unlike states where elected and appointed folks have something of a common base and friendship, there is no commonality. Presidential appointees spend an average of only three years in cabinet and subcabinet positions, all the time trying to assert themselves (i.e., exercise their power). Since no one is going to be around that long, cheap shots against others are inexpensive and are the name of the Washington game. Try being the first chairman of a new regulatory commission having no connection, no commonality, not knowing anyone working with you, not having hired any of them, and having no real authority other than to approve travel expense for the other four commissioners.

Media coverage of agencies and commissions is negligible. Unlike local experience where even a Mosquito Abatement District is excoriated for meeting without public notice, big media in D.C. would rather expose "leaks," like plumbers, rather than just open the faucets by covering meetings.

Except at the CFTC (1975–1979), to attend a multimember regulatory commission meeting such as the SEC, you had to enter at a special desk, sign in, report your name and affiliation, and tell why you are attending, i.e., who you represent—and be searched. At the CFTC you could be searched but you just walked into the meetings, were given the agenda and all (nonenforcement) agenda documents, and allowed to speak on items. Unheard of in D.C., and instantly changed the day I left the commission. Can you imagine, under our FOI laws in California being asked as a condition of entry why you want to attend a public meeting? Only in Washington.

Importantly, there is a need to recognize that the Futures Exchanges are the biggest insurance markets in the world. This is mostly a global market; prices are affected globally. "Speculators" are needed; they bid daily and whether they are buying or selling, they are providing price insurance. Everybody—buyers and sellers of all commodities, now including almost all financial instruments—hedges their costs/prices against the later ultimate actual cost of the commodity itself, billions per day. This is pure and simple risk insurance, often now required as a condition of product or production financings.

A most recent and relevant market example comes from the airline industry, really hurt by fuel costs. A few carriers, Southwest being the prime example, bought oil futures in 2007 at $70 per barrel, locking in their cost and thus hedging 2008 $130–$140 prices. Some oil producers also locked in their selling price at $70, thus "selling" cost insurance but being assured of no price reduction. Southwest won and they "lost" but each had price insurance.

6. The Birth of the CFTC

The United States Commodity Futures Trading Commission (CFTC, 1975) and the original Swiss Commodities Association (SCA, 1979), which today is the Swiss Futures and Options Association, SFOA, were both inspired in the same decade and they grew up together. I like to say the SCA actually may have been sired by the CFTC. Let me explain that last remark.

It was 1979 and I was serving as the first chairman of the CFTC. The U.S. ambassador to Switzerland invited me to speak at the Bern Residence. About 75 to 100 professionals gathered at the ambassador's residence for a luncheon. We had follow-up meetings and dinners, including meetings in Zurich. Swiss professionals complained that they could not follow all of the new processes and regulations emanating from the new CFTC. Somehow we were mailing our publications by slow boat rather than by air mail! Ferdinand "Bob" Prizi told me that. Swiss leaders, I am sure, had the same idea but I did say, "You should start an association so that we can communicate with each other." So it seems that the ambassador and those Swiss Commodity leaders spawned the association in 1979. I like to think of myself as perhaps a godfather but certainly a catalyst who was lucky enough to be on the scene 30 years ago.

Incidentally, while I flew from Washington, D.C., to Geneva, my bags flew to Boston—I met and spoke in my shabby traveling clothes. Also, after gathering my baggage, I flew to Hong Kong and Japan to pay a visit to the Japanese Commodity Federation—they were just opening themselves to world commodity trading. Yes, 19 hours on a coach-class flight—and I was criticized in Washington, D.C., for "flying around the world at government expense!"

More important is the story of the growth and, if you will, the legitimization of the commodity futures industry. I fully believe that the CFTC was the genesis of this worldwide growth and acceptance, and the original Swiss Commodities Association launched that acceptance by helping professionalize the industry.

The U.S. Congress passed the CFTC Act in October 1974 to replace a tiny bureau within the U.S. Department of Agriculture, the Commodity Exchange Authority. The CEA "regulated" trading only in agricultural commodities actually named by U.S. statues, i.e., soy beans and sow bellies and other named farm products. The CEA had been orphaned in the basement of the United States Department of Agriculture building in Washington, D.C. It had about 20 staff members in D.C. and intercom communication was by a 1920s buzzer system. In Chicago, the CEA office was in the basement of the Board of Trade. The tenant was trying to regulate the landlord.

The "Old Guard," mostly from the Chicago Board of Trade, were opposed to what they thought would be more regulation, but masterful leadership from Leo Melamed of the Chicago Mercantile Exchange encouraged Congress—led by its agricultural committees—to craft the act. The omnibus all-inclusive definition of a commodity was adopted: "Any item of goods or service that is traded on an exchange." The act also preempted the various state regulatory bodies, which led to abuses in so-called "London Options." The CFTC simply was not constituted and did not have staff to chase these abusive off-exchange cold call telephonic naked option sellers.

Those first days of a new regulatory commission were, indeed, hectic. The act, passed in October 1974, provided that it go into effect six months later—on Monday, April 21, 1975. Because of delays, the President Ford-appointed commission was not sworn-in and could not operate until Wednesday, April 16. We had two days to promulgate the first commission order—to "license" existing exchanges and trading. This initial regulatory order was delivered to the Federal Register at 1:50 p.m. Friday, April 18 (by two SEC lawyers whom we had recruited) to be printed in the Monday Federal Register. Had we missed the 2 p.m. print deadline, the markets would have not been able to open on the following Monday!

Those first days and months were also made difficult because we were new to the legal world. There was no body of court case law. We had to establish Appellate Court precedent before we could obtain injunctions against the illegal "London Option" operators and others. The exchanges, however, were most cooperative. We issued a series of market-place rules and regulations—extant today—and the market professionals complied. Contrary to some earlier beliefs, we established a market-friendly commission. And did the markets grow!

Massive exponential volume growth followed our authorization of new markets, including those in interest rates, currencies, and in basic financial futures. The first U.S. venture into financial futures, led by Melamed, began at the CME's International Money Market about two years prior to the birth of the CFTC. Next came T-bill futures, approved by the CFTC and the U.S. Treasury. Then came Ginnie Mae mortgage futures at the CBOT. Earlier, the U.S. Securities and Exchange Commission shunted aside futures overtures to assume jurisdiction. But when the CFTC approved mortgage futures, we were immediately challenged by the Securities and Exchange Commission staff, they claiming this was their turf (I had to find and talk to Rod Hills, SEC chairman, to stop a threatened suit: *SEC vs. CFTC*). The rest is history. Again, the CFTC led the way for a major new institutionalized financial futures market. Again; industry leaders in our exchanges (notably the Chicago Mercantile Exchange) were ready to implement progress in the market place. Incidentally, and as an aside, the Ginnie Mae contract never worked out and was de-listed. However, the CBOT tried U.S. 30-year bond futures, which worked famously well.

Still, there were some who would try to defy the most basic market limit regulations, epitomized by the Hunt brothers' families. Acknowledging the established three million bushel soybean limit, the brothers simply and very simplistically had nine family members each take a three million bushel position—and this at the end of the harvest season with storage at its capacity. Even after the CFTC-enforced soybean compliance, the Hunts continued their exploits, effectively cornering silver futures—at least for a short time.

Happily and quite logically, all of this has now settled down. In a cooperative mode, a 1979 CFTC action chartered the National Futures Association to create a separate, omnibus industry self-regulatory body. The NFA has performed admirably ever since as the front line of regulation backed up by a strong CFTC when necessary. The markets have matured. They are accepted and respected in the United States and in most of our trading world where collectively they perform a needed ongoing economic

24. Bill Bagley in front of a wall plaque with one of his favorite quotations, from an 1866 New York legal opinion: "No man's life, liberty, or property are safe while the legislature is in session."

function. In one sense, futures have become the biggest insurance market in the world. Again we, the CFTC and the original Swiss Commodities Association, were fortunate to be there in the beginning—in the 1970s.

Markets and trade have been the basis not just for early trade route commerce but as building blocks for world cooperation. Now, as we enter this new century of instant global communication, perhaps—just perhaps—fair and accessible global markets will become the basis of global understanding, global civility, and—maybe—a lasting peace around the world. That day will come.

I should add that prior to April 1975, I had no knowledge of or affinity with commodity futures. President Ford's staff—actually my friend, then Chief of Staff Don Rumsfeld—recommended me because I was in no way connected to the industry.

Postscript: A Unique Honor

This publication was not intended to be about Bill Bagley personally, but this postscript is hard to resist: one from a *San Francisco Chronicle* editorial and another from the Capitol *Morning Report*.

The following editorial was published in the *San Francisco Chronicle* on March 7, 2003. Titled "A Golden Bear of a Man," the piece marks the occasion when Bill Bagley was named UC Alumnus of the Year:

> William Bagley is a good-humored member of a nearly extinct species in California: a moderate Republican who gets along with Democrats—in fact, with almost any reasonable person, no matter where they fall on the political spectrum.
>
> The grandson of an Italian sea captain who jumped ship in San Francisco, Bagley served with distinction in the state Legislature for 14 years. He was appointed by President Ford to be the first Chairman of the Commodity Futures Trading Commission, and later was appointed by Gov. George Deukmejian to the University of California Board of Regents.
>
> In the state Assembly, he stood up to Gov. Ronald Reagan when he [Reagan] wanted to do away with the Rumford Fair Housing Act. Bagley tried to prevent the U.C. Regents from banning Affirmative Action in 1995, and worked to get them to rescind the ban six years later.
>
> Bagley graduated from UC Berkeley in 1949, and from Boalt Hall in 1952. Tonight he'll be honored at a gala dinner as U.C. Berkeley's Alumnus of the Year. The honor is well deserved. The university is a better institution, and California is a better place to live, because of Bill Bagley."

And this excerpt from the Capitol *Morning Report*, printed in the June 7, 2002 edition:

Bill Cavala, Director of the Speaker's Office of Majority Services, a partisan Democrat, was asked of Bill Bagley, and said: "I've known a thousand Democrats who were better than 'Bags,' but he is the best damn Republican I've ever met. He is brilliant, inexhaustively funny. His long list of legislation opening government business to the public would be legacy enough to guarantee greatness."

See the Afterword for the list.

25. Assemblyman John T. Knox (D-Richmond), a colleague and author of monumental legislation who served for 20 years, from 1960 to 1980, and then joined the Nossaman law firm.

Afterword: The Hon. John T. Knox

With a commentary about my colleague and friend for 50 years, John T. Knox, a law partner for 25.

The trust and collegiality developed among legislators—before "reform"— helped develop major pieces of legislation formulated by years of effort and compromise. This is epitomized by Assemblyman John T. (Jack) Knox (D-Richmond). He was elected in 1960, and after gathering trust among members, he produced a continuing flow of major, new legislation—even rewriting entire codes—until he left service in 1980.

As a Republican from Marin and Sonoma counties who was also elected in 1960, I observed with pride the effort and product of my friend Jack, later my law partner (now retired) in our national Nossaman law firm. In the list that follows, note indicated authorship (*JTK*) and some of my own work (*WTB*).

All—again, all—of these major statutes and codes were developed by seasoned legislators and passed with bipartisan cooperation and votes— without partisan staff instruction on "how to vote"!

The Golden Years Record

The Golden Years Record is a listing, admittedly selective, of key new legislation, 1950–1970: This is illustrative of why the California Legislature was named (by a Ford Foundation-sponsored entity) as the number one state legislature in the nation (1969–1970). Imagine today, being number one!

1. Dawning of the Civil Rights Era:

Unruh Civil Rights Act—public accommodation (1959); Fair Employment Practices Act—commission enforced (1959); Rumford Fair Housing Act (1963), reinstatement after repeal (*WTB*, 1967); Therapeutic Abortion Act—signed by Gov. Reagan (1967); Consenting Adult Act, criminal codes repeal.

2. Education:

Massive university and state college construction; Higher Education Master Plan (1959–1960); K-12 per student district equalization (1970+); UC Regents reform, governance, open meetings (*WTB*, 1968–1970); local education bond issues—66 and two-thirds percent reduced to 55% vote (1970).

3. Environmental:

Bay Conservation and Development Commission (BCDC), (*JTK*, 1965–1970); California Environmental Quality Act (CEQA), (*JTK*, 1970); funding for California Coastal Commission (*WTB*,1970–1971).

4. Taxation:

"Reagan" two billion dollar tax reform, massively progressive rates (*WTB*, 1970–1971); eliminate Business Inventory Property Tax (*WTB*, 1970–1971); institute Income Tax Withholding (*WTB*, 1971); repeal politically appointed tax appraisers (*WTB*, 1967–1968).

5. Infrastructure—Transportation/Water:

California Water Plan, $1.75 billion (1959–1960), massive storage and water transfer bond issue; statewide highway and bridge projects; create the Department of Transportation; Porter Cologne Water Act; authorize Bay Area Rapid Transit, sales tax (1961), plus other local transit districts; creation of multiple finance authorities—billions in bonds for health, housing, other infrastructures (*JTK*,1970+); reform Golden Gate Bridge governance—elected officials on Board (*WTB*, 1968).

26. *A letter from Bagley noting, "I never have opposed a bill by Jack Knox and I never will." Although of opposite parties, Bagley and Knox were fast friends and worked together on many pieces of legislation.*

6. Welfare/Health:

Massive liberal rewrite of welfare laws (1961–1963, AB69, Aid to Families); Child Protective Acts; Institute Medi-Cal (1965); Lanterman/ Petris Mental Health Act; Knox/Keene Act, authorizing HMO structure (*JTK*); Reagan "$2 billion dollar" welfare reform (*WTB*, 1971–1972).

7. General Civil Law:

New Corporate Securities Law (*JTK*, 1967); entire revision, Corporations Code (*JTK*, 1967–1977); new Partnership Act, new Non-Profit Acts (*JTK*), No-Fault Divorce (1968); entire code rewrites—evidence code, etc.

8. Governmental Processes/Municipal Law:

Omnibus constitutional revision (1966); property appraisal equalization (*JTK*, local appraisal scandals); Local Agency Formation Commission (LAFCO)—(*JTK*, regulate annexations); Ralph M. Brown Local Meeting Act (1953); Bagley/Keene State Meeting Act (*WTB*, 1967); Omnibus Open Public Records Act (*WTB*, 1968); public meeting places, no sex discrimination (*WTB*, 1970); constitutional right of privacy (1970).

A significant majority of the above-mentioned landmark statutes was the product of long-serving members and committee chairmen and staff, negotiated with stakeholders and lobbyists and/or developed by special subject-matter Select Committees—all before term limits decimated the process.

When I write about Jack Knox's legislative accomplishments, the mention of an "entire rewrite of the Corporations Code" evokes questions—how does one get to rewrite an entire code, 1965–1975?

A legislator with the ear of the Speaker or President Pro Tem, by going through the respective Rules Committees, creates a Select or Special Committee on the overall subject; the creating resolution authorizes a public advisory committee (to be appointed by the new chairman of the new Special Committee); and a modicum of money is authorized for staff and travel. Jack Knox did just that re the Corporations Code, with Bar Association support.

Harold Marsh of the Nossaman law firm was recruited as a major scrivener of/for the advisory committee. The Special Committee even had a headquarters in the then Nossaman office in Los Angeles. This was circa 1967–1969. Over the next 10 years or so, the group literally rewrote the whole code, plus partnership provisions and the nonprofit law, placed the work into bill form, and then navigated it to passage by Jack.

Adding my six bits: I was the chairman of the Assembly Judiciary Committee in 1967–1968. We passed Jack's first part rewrite—the Corporate Securities Act, Corp. Code, sec. 25,000 et seq.

Another two bits: I initiated creation of my own Special Committee on "Statewide Information Policy," appointed an advisory committee, hired Vic Fazio as staff (later he was third in line to be Speaker of the House in D.C.), and produced six products (of which I authored five)—four freedom of information laws and two constitutional amendments:

1. The Bagley Keene State Open Meeting Law (1967), which applies to over 300 state boards, agencies, and commissions;

2. The omnibus California Public Records Act (1968) opening state and local governmental records never theretofore defined;

3. The new News Shield Privilege Law (1972) applying the privilege to all subpoena-issuing bodies or agencies, not just courts;

4. The "Tracy Wood" Provision (1970), which prohibits public meetings in facilities that discriminate. Tracy Wood was a U.P.I. reporter who was not allowed to cover a meeting being held in the Sutter Club, which then excluded women until 5 p.m.;

5. The University of California Regents Open Meeting Act (1969), a constitutional amendment approved by the electorate, November 1970;

6. A "Right of Privacy," proposed by the then young Vic Fazio and added to the state constitution (1970)—later interpreted by the California Supreme Court to guarantee a woman's right of choice in California regardless of federal law, i.e., the possible reversal of *Roe v. Wade*.

This is how it was done, but now with six-year term limits, members could not even start such a process.

Biography

Bill Bagley is a people person personified. He spent much of the past 50 years in *pro bono* public service, all the while practicing law in California and in Washington, D.C., with the nationwide Nossaman Law Firm, since 1981.

Working his way through school as a summer firefighter, he graduated *Phi Beta Kappa* from the University of California in 1949. He was the valedictorian and permanent president of his class of 5,000 and was an editor of the *California Law Review*, Boalt Hall, 1952.

He writes with a wealth of personal knowledge of the Golden Years, hoping that the ways and means, the methods and successes of that era (1950–1970) will inspire today's officeholders and thoughtful leaders to repair what has become a partisan-driven, a gridlock-plagued, and at times just plain dysfunctional legislature with a term-limited vision. "Present members think that's the way it always was, that's the way it works."

Elected as a Republican to the Assembly from Marin and Sonoma Counties in 1960 at the age of 32, Bill spent 14 years in the California Legislature. He chaired five major committees under both Democratic and Republican Speakers, and authored more than 500 pieces of legislation, including major civil rights and open government programs, major tax and welfare reforms, and many civil law changes while serving on the Judiciary Committee for 14 years.

Then, successively, he was appointed the first chairman of the Commodity Futures Trading Commission (President Ford, 1975–1979), member of the California Public Utilities Commission, and then member and chairman of the California Transportation Commission (Gov. Deukmejian, 1983–1989), and member of the UC Board of Regents (Gov. Deukmejian, 1989–2002). He was named the UC Alumnus of the Year, 2003—a true "Old Blue" Golden Bear.